To the Desert and Back

Philip Mirvis

Karen Ayas

George Roth

To the Desert and Back

The Story of One of the Most Dramatic Business Transformations on Record

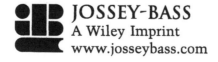
JOSSEY-BASS
A Wiley Imprint
www.josseybass.com

Published by Jossey-Bass
A Wiley Imprint
989 Market Street, San Francisco, CA 94103-1741   www.josseybass.com

Jossey-Bass books and products are available through most bookstores. To contact Jossey-Bass directly call our Customer Care Department within the U.S. at 800-956-7739, outside the U.S. at 317-572-3986 or fax 317-572-4002.

Jossey-Bass also publishes its books in a variety of electronic formats. Some content that appears in print may not be available in electronic books.

Library of Congress Cataloging-in-Publication Data

Mirvis, Philip H., 1951-
   To the desert and back : the story of one of the most dramatic business transformations on record / by Philip Mirvis, Karen Ayas, George Roth.
      p. cm.
Includes bibliographical references and index.
   ISBN: 978-0-470-62692-4
   1. Unilever N.V.   2. Food industry and trade—Netherlands.   3. Consolidation and merger of corporations—Netherlands—Case studies.   4. Corporate reorganizations—Netherlands—Case studies.   5. International business enterprises—Case studies.
I. Ayas, Karen.   II. Roth, George, 1957-   III. Title.
   HD9015.N44U535 2003
   338.7'61664'009492—dc21

                                                                                    2003002023

FIRST EDITION
HB Printing   10 9 8 7 6 5 4 3 2 1

Contents

Part V: Transfer

Part VI: Takeaways for Leading Change

Preview: The View
from the Desert

Our little caravan grew self-conscious, and fell dead
quiet, afraid and ashamed to flaunt its smallness in
the presence of the stupendous hills.
—*T. E. Lawrence*, Seven Pillars of Wisdom

Camel caravans carrying two hundred riders converge from six directions in the desert. This is Wadi Rum, the Valley of the Moon—ancient passageway of East–West traders and scene of Lawrence of Arabia's most haunting memories. It is a broad, dry valley, a scrubby desertscape, punctuated with alleyways formed by towering red sandstone mountains, natural rock bridges, and rose-colored sand dunes. Though many have tried, no one has described it more lyrically than Lawrence:[1]

> The crags were capped in nests of domes, less hotly red than the body of the hill; rather grey and shallow. They gave the finishing semblance of Byzantine architecture to this irresistible place: this processional way greater than imagination. The Arab armies would have been lost in the length and breadth of it, and within the walls a squadron of aeroplanes could have wheeled in formation.

The caravans gathering in this desert do not transport Arab armies or nomad tribes who still live in this unforgettable land. Astride the camels are tribes of modern-day traders, assembled here for a leadership retreat. They are Dutch businesspeople—180 of them plus assorted consultants, event support staff, and guides.

While in this desert, like thousands of traders and tourists before them, they will explore its vast beauty and make the journey to Petra, some seventy-five kilometers to the northwest. They also have come to this place to survey a landscape of their own making.

For the next three days, they will explore their business and personal histories, their triumphs and failures, their individual and team relationships, and trek forward through their visions for the future of their company. Nestled in niches in rocky cliffs, walking or riding in Jeeps through the rosy sand, crouching around fires in the desert night, they will laugh, cry, reminisce quietly, argue, and shout in anger.

They are here to translate their experience from the last five years into a vision for the next five. They are here to reinvent themselves—again.

Capitalism and Contemplation

The scene in the desert of Wadi Rum is but one in a five-year drama played out in the Dutch food business of Unilever, the giant Anglo-Dutch foods and home and personal care products business.[2] With products from tea and ice cream to shampoo and toothpaste, Unilever owns some of the world's best-known brands—Lipton, Hellmann's, Ragu, Rama, Magnum, Bertolli, Knorr, Bird's Eye, Slim-Fast, Dove, Ponds, Signal, Close-up, Surf, and Omo, to name just a few. It employs more than 265,000 workers in more than five hundred companies in ninety countries worldwide and does business in another seventy. Its foods business is the world's largest after Nestlé.

When the story opens in 1995, the setting is Oss, in the southern part of Holland. There, Unilever's Dutch meat, sauce, and soup business is in deep trouble, foundering financially and staring down ever-shrinking markets. Workers and management alike are mired in a deadening culture: the job in the factory is to mind your own business; in the corner office, to make the numbers no matter what. Little thought to product quality. Less thought to shareholder value. No thought to growing the business. South Holland is twenty years behind the times. The factories, probably forty.

What unfolds in the five-year trip from Oss to Wadi Rum is the transformation of that business—and eventually of Unilever itself. As in many stories of reinvention, the plotline is simple: the old ways buried, a new organization born. What makes Unilever's to-the-desert-and-back story stand out? First, this business's efforts to change and grow succeed—dramatically, more than once. Second, they are done on a massive scale—this story reaches from outlying factories all the way to HQ, it involves thousands of workers and nearly two hundred team leaders, it galvanizes both mindsets and "heartsets," changing both the business and personal lives of all the players. And there is more.

The Story Behind the Story

The basic story describes how a workforce and its leaders created growth, energized a market, and brought new spirit to a traditional and tired organization. It sounds like hundreds of so-called business biographies that have come before, but it is not.

"Describing how we achieved double-digit growth is not easy," says a commercial manager from one of the business units involved:

> It is about paradoxes: planning and luck, teams and individuals, great ideas and small steps, far-reaching ambition and everyday realism, being bold and being humble, through chaos and organization. Maybe we can say it was "passion for winning."

Growth and transformation, paradox and passion: standard vocabulary for business success stories throughout the United States, Europe, and Asia. And much of the action here looks at first like a set piece of twenty-first-century business and culture change: restructuring, asset sales, staff reductions, stretch targets, staff training, team building, new types of management meetings, and on and on.

It is the story behind the story that makes this one compelling. It is the way all the plans, visions, intentions, and actions are combined and integrated into a top-to-bottom, wall-to-wall transformation that grabs our attention and helps produce the successful conclusion. In the end, growth becomes the core purpose of the business, in the face of mature, seemingly no-growth markets. And growth, in business and personal terms, becomes the standard by which all employees— from the director's offices to the factory floor—judge themselves.

The most dramatic transformation on record? Surely not because of the size of the business (one part of a global company) or even the growth in sales (unexpected as it was). Indeed, this sounds like hype to the Dutch who are sensitive to showiness.[3] We've billed it as such because of the human drama of changed lives and horizons and because of the conscious effort that was made to dramatize events in the company and transform everyday business into theater.

Sneak Preview

Also, this is an inside story—told in large part by the people who took part in it, from all quarters of the company, in their own words, on the record.[4] We were present for most of it and later did exhaustive research to help create the "learning history" that institutionalized this business story for this company. In our retelling here, we try to help you understand the heart and soul beneath this company's setbacks and achievements.

In Part I: Turnaround, Unilever sends a turnaround king and a hard-bitten factory manager to its moribund, backwater meat, sauce, and soup business in South Holland to shake things up or shut it down. What's really wrong here? What can be done to grab the attention of the cynical, unionized workers and complacent old-line management? After waking it up and tearing it apart, how can new leaders possibly put this losing business back together again, never mind make it grow?

Part II: Takeover shifts the scene from Oss to Rotterdam, home of Unilever's Dutch HQ and its larger, more successful foods and spreads business, now targeted for a merger with the backwater business from the South. The merger scene and its aftermath have all the earmarks of a classic culture clash—plenty of resistance and denial, creative and not-so-creative tension, winners and losers, rejoicing and pain. Now the action is very, very visible to the Unilever brass, who see young up-and-comers instigate what amounts to a revolution in one of the units. That's not all. Disruption, ambiguity, and anxiety reign. Many wonder, Whose side are you on? What can possibly rise from this chaos? And how will we find fresh purpose and spirit?

These questions are partly answered in Part III: Transforming the Organization. Here the theme of developing people and teams takes the spotlight. We see how a huge, innovative leadership structure for the company takes form—180 leaders in all! They now have the brief not only to run the business from day to day but also to take a key role in developing people's mindsets and heartsets for moving it forward on its path to growth. Not without resistance and pain, they begin to appreciate the value of revealing their emotions and personal aspirations to their cohorts at work, and they learn new ways to think and talk about the business, their teams, and themselves. Lurking in the shadows surrounding the advances made by all this team building are the cynics, the skeptics, and the fearful. What does all this talk about connecting and community really mean? Why the travel to visit faraway places and the all-company gatherings to play games? Why should we go along this time, when so many failed innovations have gone before? And isn't it all rather cultlike, anyway, with special language, team flags, and folderol?

Part III takes the people development, team training, and community-building thread of the story to about mid-1999. In Part IV: Transforming the Business, we start with a bit of a flashback to describe in more depth how the different operating units began to reshape themselves, expand their offerings, and change long-standing work practices and traditional relationships with their employees and markets.

Here is where the business nitty-gritty of the drama unfolds. How will one unit develop new products, enter new markets, and exploit new channels to grow by 13 percent in 1999? How will another—after years of decline—stabilize volumes, increase market share, grow several of its brands, and dramatically redefine its relationships with retailers and consumers? How will some of the factories improve efficiencies from 60 percent to more than 80 percent and shrink trading losses dramatically? And how will they all adapt the company's movement toward linking business and personal achievements, making that link apparent in the ongoing operation of the business? The answers to all these questions form the story line for Part IV of the book.

Part V: Transfer picks up where we began this introduction: in the desert of Wadi Rum in Jordan in early 2000. On that trip to the desert, the curtain falls on one act of this transformation drama and rises on another as the 180 leaders recount how they changed and grew the business, their teams, and themselves over the last five years and explain what their visions for future growth hold. In the end, the ways they transfer the lessons they learned and spread their legacy of growth form a never-ending story . . . so the last chapter takes us back to Rotterdam and on to Singapore, where the first scenes in the next act begin to play.

The last part of the book moves outside the action, beyond the story. In Part VI: Takeaways for Leading Change, we throw off the role of observers and reporters and sometime participants in the drama. Now we are more like teachers or guides as we suggest ways to analyze and understand what happened in the Unilever story. What lessons might other organizations glean from Unilever's trip to the desert? What made these hard and soft changes work in this particular company at this particular time? How might they be replicated in other places? Can this approach to organizational change succeed on a smaller scale—and in settings closer to home?

In the end, the answers lie not so much in our theories and analysis as in really seeing and feeling what this company experienced. And the best way to "experience their experience" is to go straight into the action and behind the scenes yourself.

Part I

Turnaround

Chapter 1

Wake-Up Call

If you ask every single employee who was there
what day they remember best, they will all say that
Friday in 1995 at the warehouse.

—Plant operator

In the spring of 1995, the fourteen hundred employees of Unilever Vlees Groupe Nederland (UVGN) assembled in the early morning at their factories and boarded motor buses for a field trip. Their destination? Unknown. The purpose of the trip? Top secret.

"I thought we were going on a trip to the Efteling amusement park or even to Disneyland," said one of UVGN's machine operators. Instead they arrived at a warehouse, where they were greeted by recently appointed UVGN manufacturing director Hans Synhaeve and the company's brand new chairman, Tex Gunning.

Inside, 3,700 pallets of rejected goods towered in stacks from floor to ceiling. The warehouse reeked with the nauseating smell of rotten food. As far as the eye could see—left, right, front, back— were piles of products unfit for sale: spoiled sausages in defective tins and vacuum packs, leaking cans of soups and sauces, poorly sealed packages of dry soup and sauce mixes. Products worth 9 million guilders, the equivalent of 4.3 million euros. Ready for destruction.

When the sight and stench of the warehouse of waste had begun to sink in, Gunning started to talk. As a production line worker recalls, "He spoke very quietly in the beginning, but in the end gave us hell." Then managers and accountants, quality experts and production workers walked aisle after aisle counting cans, calculating the money lost, and contemplating the waste of their time and talent. Later, a parade of forklifts trucked the pallets outside to a large, lined pit, where the worthless goods were unceremoniously dumped in and covered with earth.

The idea that UVGN had such massive product quality problems came as a complete surprise to most employees. "We had no idea what we were doing," said one factory worker. "We thought that everything that we made was good. We had no idea that the rejects were so much. We didn't know. We made the numbers."

And most in management just kept their eyes on the books, where they could point to profits year after year. But profitability told only part of the tale, and this day in UVGN's warehouse of waste was the beginning of Unilever's trip to the desert and back.

A Sinking Ship

UVGN had been formed in 1970 with the merger of meat butchering and exporting businesses dating back more than 150 years. Located in Oss, in southern Holland, the company operated both as a sourcing unit and trading unit in 1995. The sourcing unit included four factories: meat, soups, sauces, and dry mixes. The trading unit sold branded products through Dutch retailers. UVGN's primary brand—Unox—was the oldest and largest food brand in Holland, an emblem of traditional Dutch food values.

When Unilever veteran Hans Synhaeve entered the scene as the new manufacturing director in spring 1995 and was joined by Gunning two months later, they found a company in deep trouble: lower and lower volumes since 1991, no increases in market share, shrinking margins, and higher costs year after year. Profits maintained through repeated price increases. Accounting cleverness concealing true financial performance. A product portfolio overloaded with offerings in low-growth, low-profit market segments. Major money lost making junk. That wasn't all. Competition from CPC and Honig, as well as from private labels such as grocer Albert Heijn, was getting stiffer. And competitors like Campbell's and Heinz were showing their shareholders double-digit growth.

Minding Their Own Business

To make matters worse, UVGN had issued four product recalls since 1993—traced to key missing ingredients, improper storage, faulty packaging, and the like. Canned beef that had been adulterated with pork. The fresh meat *theeworst* was missing a key preservative. The most visible recall was the result of microscopic leakage in the family-size cans of Unox pea soup, the brand's flagship product. It had almost prompted the closure of the Oss factory.

As product quality rejection rates climbed, a team of factory managers began turning some rejected products into seconds—and a phalanx of workers was employed just to cut the brand labels off the cans of still-edible soups and sausages so they could be sold at a discount through the company store. Demand couldn't keep up with the supply of rejects and write-offs mounted. No one in UVGN had calculated the profits lost from manufacturing and selling second-versus first-quality goods. And no one asked for the figures. The norm was for factory workers to mind their own business while managers kept their distance from subordinates and superiors alike. When a plant supervisor went to his boss one year to say that he could not accept a bonus because there had been a major loss due to leakage in smoked pork sausage packaging (equal to 2 percent of total volume), the boss replied: "Your responsibility is to run your line, ours is to take care of the quality." In other words, Don't question the system, just do your job.

On the Verge of Death

It was a company "in need of radical change," said Synhaeve, "a company that no longer reacted. I saw there was sufficient critical mass of good people, but they needed to be wakened up, as they were partly dead."

With management's attention fixated on profitability, there naturally was no forward-looking vision or strong strategic direction. People development was virtually ignored. The new product pipeline was dry. Major restructurings and downsizings had followed one after another since the 1970s, dramatically changing the character of the company—the slaughterhouses and crews of manual labor were gone, and total employment had declined from seven thousand workers to roughly fourteen hundred by 1995. Still, employment was seen as a lifelong proposition for the company's employees, many of whom joined as early as age fourteen and expected to stay until retirement.

Coping with dramatic changes in consumer trends and the constant pressure to maintain profitability had left the company depleted. "Most of the management board were frustrated," said one account manager, "and they showed it. They were not a team. There were some older guys, near the end of their career at Unilever. There was one hands-on manager, always eating a sausage. He died of a heart attack. A typical head office guy, sitting in his office all day, replaced him."

Unilever HQ took notice. UVGN was targeted for immediate turnaround or, failing that, would be put up for sale. The immediate challenge, as one insider put it, was "to prevent the ship from sinking." An alarm needed to sound—and loudly. And the new leaders knew just how to get people's attention.

Enter the New Chairman

Right from the start, it was clear that the new chairman would be different from his predecessor. Though an economist by training and a Unilever veteran, Gunning was no bean-counter or classic corporate man. "When I saw the new chairman at the farewell speech for the old chairman," recalled one manager, "I thought, hey, things are going to change. It was very clear."

Louis Willem "Tex" Gunning was born in 1950 in the Netherlands.[1] His youthful biography includes what historians have identified as archetypal characteristics of future leaders: death of a father at an early age, love for one caregiver/hate for the other, early defiance of authority, and bouts of rebelliousness (see spotlight).[2]

Gunning's business career started in the late 1970s when he joined Peat, Marwick Auditing and then moved into their strategic consulting services operation. In 1983, he joined Unilever in the Controller's Department and moved to the controller's office of its Dutch food subsidiary Van den Bergh/Jurgens in 1984. His horizons broadened in 1987 through 1989, when he served in the secretariat of Unilever's special committee of managing directors. "Working for Floris Maljers, the Dutch chairman at the time, changed my life," he recalled. "I met somebody who was so much smarter than me and so worldly. I realized that I had to work harder on myself and read much more about philosophy and history." His time at the secretariat exposed him to the full scope of the company's operations and enabled him to meet its top executives.

Spotlight: Tex Gunning

As he put it, Tex's childhood got off to a "rocky start" in 1952, when he was two years old, and his father was killed in the Korean War. With two young children to take care of, his distraught mother remarried within two years. What warmth there was to be found did not come from his stepfather but from his mother, some extended family members, and a few friends.

Escalating hostilities made Tex's mother insist, at great personal expense, that her children be protected by moving them to boarding school. A uninspired student in secondary school, he excelled in mathematics but chafed at the seeming arbitrariness of school leaders and teachers. After graduation, he had to combine studies and work to pay for his living and fees at the Erasmus University in Rotterdam.

With military service compulsory in the Netherlands, Gunning followed his father's example and joined the Dutch Marines. The sense of adventure was exhilarating but the culture of the military proved too confining for the free-spirited recruit. One evening, when decorum called for the marines to appear in "dress blues," he showed up in blue jeans, got into a scrape, and was granted dismissal from the service. "I learned an enormous lesson from this," he remembered, "I didn't accomplish anything by just fighting against the system. I would have to do things differently in corporate life."

A marathon runner and avid reader of management books and classics in psychology and philosophy, Gunning is described, by one observer, as "lean, boyish, but otherwise unremarkable" in physical appearance.[3] What is distinctive about him is that he is "always trying to learn and deal with current issues." He faced plenty of them when taking charge of UVGN.

Joining Hans

As Unilever's trip to the desert and back begins, Gunning is back in his homeland from his tours as commercial director of Unilever Thailand and then managing director of the company's foods businesses in Australia. Fresh from six years abroad, he is full of new ideas about the business and a restless ambition to get things done. He is in the factories at all hours, inviting everyday workers to important meetings and events, and often dressing in blue jeans rather than the corporate suit.

While extremely demanding and intellectually challenging, Gunning is soon sized up as someone very unlike the typical Unilever executive—"a man for everybody," as one manager put it. "He understands the problems and he is connected to work levels. He knows people by name. He knows the issues and you can talk with him. Most chairmen just sit in their corner office and you see them twice, when they come in and when they say good-bye."

It helps a lot that Hans Synhaeve is already on board when Tex arrives—if Gunning is to captain a sinking ship, he will need the advantage of having an experienced first mate on board. A little older and already known at UVGN as a "factory guy" through and through, Hans is the perfect foil for the youngish-looking new chairman, who has no hands-on factory experience to match his reputation—and plans—for turning things around.

With Hans as his partner—once the initial shock wore off—Tex quickly established his credibility with managers and workers alike. They felt they knew what he was saying and his intentions behind what he did. They believed he cared about the company, about growing it, about people's jobs, people's feelings. The effect was palpable. Still, there were doubts and reservations. Said one laboratory manager:

> I work here twenty-six years and have seen five or six chairman. So, I thought, here comes another one. We have had so many before him. . . . But Tex grasped my attention. He would talk for three hours and I would be listening breathlessly and think about it. He knew how to motivate us. But, on the other hand, we distrusted him a little: nice talk, but can you live up to what you say?

Keeping the Ship Afloat

The surreal scene in the warehouse of waste was a theatrical way to sound a powerful wake-up call—a creatively crafted mix of hard facts and figures with expressive sights and sounds to dramatize the daunting performance gap concealed behind the numbers. As one department manager put it, "The scene was clearly set by making it very clear that every one of us was responsible for the mess we're in. We needed to come up with a plan to generate five million in savings in three months."

Tex and Hans worked with a handpicked group to accomplish the needed savings. For months, they acted as teachers and coaches, introducing them to basic business and financial concepts. Through it all, they often spent twenty-four hours a day in the factories, walking the floors and getting fresh ideas from line workers and supervisors on how to gin up production.

But keeping the ship afloat required more than an emotional shock and bottom-up improvement in factory performance. Staffing levels—in management, office, and operating areas—had swollen to the point that UVGN could not be competitive. Restructuring was clearly necessary to get costs down further, and the fresh meat operation that over nearly two decades had become increasingly peripheral to Unilever's core food business was the obvious target. The immediate cost savings could come from closing the fresh meat factory, eliminating temporary jobs, and laying off another 350 people.

The script from the warehouse scene forward was clear: the traditional approach of raising prices rather than improving productivity was no longer viable. Productivity improvements would mean greater efficiencies, and greater efficiencies would provide higher profits. But, to grow in new areas, the company would have to shrink in others. The message that people heard was that there would be winners and losers.

Creative Destruction

The situation at UVGN was part of a much larger awakening occurring throughout Holland and much of industrialized Europe.[4] The "creative destruction" of capitalism, having swept through the United States in the quality movement and shareholder-driven downsizing of the 1980s and into Britain in the early '90s, arrived full force on the Continent mid-decade. Global giants headquartered in Holland, like Royal Dutch Shell and Philips Electronics, commenced layoffs and launched profit improvement efforts. Unilever was not immune.

While asset sales and layoffs had become rather matter-of-fact propositions in U.S. business, they were anything but that in Europe in 1995. Unilever was wary of eliminating jobs, particularly Dutch jobs, in light of its overall corporate profitability. Workers councils—state-sanctioned bodies that represented workers' interests in the factories—expected to review and rule on each personnel decision. Downsizing and restructuring under these conditions could take months, even years. And though they had been fully apprised of performance problems, the workforce was suspicious of new management's motives and vowed to keep a close eye on the process as it played out.

No one was more mindful of these dynamics and their potential consequences than Hans Cornuit, head of human resources at UVGN, who ensured that the staff reductions were properly handled. He worked with Unilever leadership to gain support for letting a group of young managers rebalance staffing plans and eliminate temporary labor. There was full disclosure of the dire financial situation of the company and honest answers to questions about which jobs were being cut and why. An attractive early retirement package was developed for older workers, and area employers were enlisted to help in the placement of laid-off employees.

Today these approaches are best practices in firms accustomed to downsizing. At the time in Holland, they were pathbreaking. And employees sensed that the days of business as usual were over.

The Organization Reborn

By January 1996, four months into the turnaround, UVGN had achieved savings of 4 million euros. Improved performance of key production lines resulted in an 18 percent increase in operating efficiencies. One line improved its efficiency from 60 percent to 80 percent in just twelve weeks. By March 1996 headcount had been reduced by five hundred.

The big changes were more than a reduced workforce and short-term performance gains. New attitudes and ambitions were emerging (Exhibit 1.1). "This marked the beginning of a new company," said one marketing manager. "It was illustrated by the way we talked about it. We told people, 'You have a job in the *new* organization.'"

"When the restructuring program was introduced our chairman went to the press," recalled an account manager.

> He invited the local paper to look at what they were doing. The headlines read, "Unox investing 150 million in its brands." Not that Unilever is going to slash jobs! It was turned around. In February we told our people that the assumption was nobody has a job unless they were placed in the new organization.

The restructuring also included delayering—eliminating managerial as well as factory floor jobs—which not only further reduced costs but had other benefits. The broad agenda of getting costs

Exhibit 1.1 In Their Own Words:
The Old and the New UGVN

OLD UVGN	NEW UVGN

On Structure . . .

Operator A: We had shift leaders, department heads, first operators, operators, and so on. I only saw my own boss. Only my boss talked to the shift leaders.

Operator A: The new leaders broke up the hierarchy. Instead of respecting the hierarchy of command, they invited people in the lower ranks to challenge top managers.

Chief engineer: The old UVGN was a functional organization with big engineering and quality departments. Production was almost a minor step in the process. Departments did not talk to each other and everything was run through the hierarchy. There was no real teamwork.

Plant Manager: We started in a situation where it was not clear who was responsible for what. Now there is a factory team responsible for everything that goes on in that factory. When there is a quality problem in production, there is absolutely no doubt who should be doing something about it. And it is *not* the quality department; it is the factory team.

On Responsibility . . .

Operator B: If a machine broke, you or the boss went to the technical people and they tried to fix it. We got to go to the canteen. You didn't have much responsibility. The boss worked in the office and we didn't see him. But we didn't care. There was always work, and there was always pay.

Sales director: If you work, you want to enjoy it, and you want a certain amount of responsibility. You just want to be part of the community. Now, people say: "It is your responsibility." And many like that. People like to have responsibility.

Operator A: The attitude was you worked for the money. You could make as much overtime as you want. It was no problem. But if you worked a little bit harder then the other guys, they called you a wanker.

Marketing manager: It was a fun atmosphere, because UVGN had changed from an unprofitable organization to a more profitable one. There was a sense of community, because the teams were small and also because of the kind of people who worked there. We were all willing to spend long hours working quite hard with a real team commitment to go for it and to make this company a success.

**Exhibit 1.1 In Their Own Words:
The Old and the New UGVN, Cont'd.**

OLD UVGN	NEW UVGN
On Management Style . . .	
Operator C: On this side of the street was the factory, across the street was the headquarters. You never saw the marketing guys on the floor and you never saw the director himself. Only when there were big problems. They gave hell to us, but otherwise you never saw them.	**Supervisor:** You are more involved in all layers. You ask, "Perhaps an operator has some ideas?" It is [a form of] recognition, although you do not earn a penny more for it. It gives more content to your work, more satisfaction. And because I am happy with my job my output will be greater.

aligned with revenues was more easily accepted by unionized workers when they saw that the consequences extended to management as well. "This time the big difference was that we saw the numbers," said a machine operator. "And we learned that layoffs were not only for the people on the floor. If people did not think it was necessary, it would never have happened, because we would have gone on strike. We do not let layoffs happen that easily. People knew that it was necessary for the future of the business and their own future."

Communications about the layoff, delayering, and asset sales, while respectful of the human cost, stressed the opportunity this gave for rebirth—for both the business and its people. Some people complained that management's actions were too tough and cavalier. And there were concerns that, according to one manager, "There was no plan for the people, the survivors, who stayed behind." On the whole, though, after the cutbacks were completed, the sentiment was that the ship was afloat and ready to move forward. The next question was, Where would it head?

Chapter 2

Rebuilding the Business

> **MEMO FROM THE OFFICE OF THE CHAIRMAN**
>
> The decision over the UVGN business has been a particularly difficult one. However, based on the performance of the recent years we have decided to sell the UVGN business. The disposal will be carried out as soon as possible. As current managers, you will be given the option to make a management buy out (MBO) and own the business. I recommend that you consider this opportunity very seriously.

In January 1996 UVGN's management team was called to the main conference room in the Head Office building in Oss. On the table in front of each of the participants was a memo from HQ Unilever announcing that UVGN was to be sold. "Unilever has decided to get rid of us," Gunning told his managers, "but you are allowed to make a preemptive offer to buy the business if you believe in it."

After ten minutes or so of discussion, the managers realized that the memo wasn't for real, though divestment was a very real possibility. To be competitive again, UVGN would have to do much more than cut costs. The business had to be rebuilt—and it had to grow.

The New Vision

As 1996 dawned, the restructuring of UVGN was all but over—at least as an intellectual matter. "It just had to be executed," said newly appointed controller Hein Swinkels, adding:

> We now needed to build the business. How are we going to grow? What went wrong in the factories was very visible. How to fix marketing and sales operations was not so tangible. We had to formulate new ideas on what to do there. Apart from some loose ideas around product categories, the chairman did not yet have a coherent strategy or vision of what to do with Unox, the brands, the product groups, etc. So we embarked upon a process to formulate that.

The scene had been set with the MBO memo at the management meeting: The UVGN managers would now have to devote themselves to the speedy development of an overall strategy for growth, with a specific program for each of the factories. Dubbed Strategic Programme 2002, the process was specifically designed to introduce UVGN managers to the latest thinking about business opportunities, customers, and organization. It also gave them new tools for analysis and a forum in which to debate ideas and test hunches about how to move the business forward. Perhaps its most distinctive feature was the unprecedented requirement for the strategic planning team to read and talk in English. "This was really unusual," one UVGN manager reported, "English became our business language."

Strategic Programme 2002

Strategic planning wasn't new to Unilever or even to UVGN, but taking a longer view—looking five years ahead—was a different way to go about it, and bringing in consultants to teach the team about strategizing, rather than do the analysis and hand them a plan, proved energizing.[1]

What's more, Strategic Programme 2002 would not rest on the usual method of extrapolating financial goals from past performance.

UVGN would start by setting an impossible final target—a doubling of shareholder value by 2002—that would force the team to scrap its current plans and rethink its entire business strategy. The new vision—to become the leading food authority in Holland by building an exciting and innovative food culture in the nation—was every bit as daunting and, at this point, unimaginable. At the same time, Synhaeve (see spotlight) and UVGN's operations managers would have to continue to deal with the aftermath of restructuring and keep a sharp focus on short-term results.

Spotlight: Hans Synhaeve

In his early forties when he was called in to UVGN, Hans Synhaeve was primarily a manufacturing specialist who was seen, according to a colleague, as "a funny little man who could not speak proper Dutch." Born in Belgium, he had started his career as an engineer in a Belgian meat factory. Since joining Unilever in 1983, he had always been in its foods business—and primarily in meat products—assuming ever bigger responsibilities on the manufacturing front as he built his track record. He was particularly known for introducing new technology and educating factory workers. In one of the factories, he quadrupled volume in a few months. In another, he dealt with serious quality problems and handled a major political strike. In 1992, he returned to the meat factory in Belgium, which was in crisis—he was given six months and full authority to accomplish a complete turnaround. When he arrived at UVGN in spring 1995, he was ready to move on to yet another, bigger challenge.

Hans embarked on the UVGN turnaround and later transformation from a production efficiency and factory point of view. While the new chairman was more the "front stage" leader who would make the case for action top-down, Hans was the roll-up-your-sleeves, backstage type who wanted to fix things from the ground up. Indeed, he was dubbed Columbo, with reference to Peter Falk's detective character, because of his ramshackle manner and his indirect but invariably effective methods for getting the job done.

From Old Logic to New Mindsets

UVGN's competitors were well ahead in responding to the financial markets. In its 1996 annual report, Campbell's had proclaimed, "The shareholder is the prime, supreme, and first of all stakeholders." Heinz reported itself "on track to deliver double-digit growth in annual earnings through 2000." And CPC International announced that it wanted "to kick the bejeebies out of its competitors when it comes to annual rewards to shareholders."

UVGN's initial five-year profitability forecasts had been NLG 300 million short of shareholder expectations. And a sobering look at current performance showed that the company was also behind in terms of controlling manufacturing costs and final product quality. The worst news of all? UVGN's key brand—Unox—successful though it still was in well-established markets, was not positioned to reach new and emerging customer segments. The mandate was clear: Building the business would require a whole new way of thinking in the company.

UVGN would have to transform its old logic into new mindsets, as sketched in Exhibit 2.1. Under the old logic, UVGN paid attention only to the existing markets of its three businesses: soups, meats, and sauces. Going forward the company would need what was termed *foresight* to see its opportunity horizons.

Exhibit 2.1 New Mindsets, New Lingo

Moving from Old Logic . . .	. . . Toward New Mindsets
Currently served markets	Opportunity horizons (foresight)
Defending today's business	Creating new competitive space
Portfolio of businesses	Portfolio of capabilities
Following consumers	Leading consumers
Maximize hit rate	Maximize learning
Commitment equals investment	Commitment equals persistence

Most Unox products, for instance, were aimed at traditional consumer segments: housewives buying goods at the grocer to take home and cook into customary Dutch meals. The strategy team looked into changing eating habits like the increasing consumption of snacks and meals-on-the-go. And they also studied the food preferences of growing consumer segments such as young single adults, students, and children. This opened up their opportunity horizons and created, in strategic parlance, new competitive space.

Consideration of consumer "need states" highlighted growing interest in healthy ingredients, in exotic dishes from foreign lands, and in "fun foods." The new mindset led managers to think more about leading their consumers, and set in motion some innovative ideas about brand extensions and entirely new product lines.

Learning Faster and Better

As the excitement grew over these ideas, UVGN managers embraced them with cautious enthusiasm. For one thing, keeping manufacturing costs and product quality under control was a continuing paramount concern. Yet, unless the company could get the growth engine going, it would not be able to survive, much less outmatch its competition and show significant gains in shareholder value.

Also, it was clear that new capabilities were needed to gain movement on the near-term initiatives, never mind the overall program. The UVGN workforce had not yet developed either the skills or the confidence to bring the vision to life. In the end, success would surely depend on UVGN's ability to grow its people. As one executive put it, "We have to compete through learning faster and better than our competitors."

Developing Highly Effective People

An important first step came in early February 1996, when twenty Unox employees went through the company's new "Covey course," a training program based on Stephen Covey's personal development best-seller, *The Seven Habits of Highly Effective People*,[2] delivered by the U.K. branch of the Learning Company. Hans Cornuit (see spotlight) and a number of managers were certified as Covey trainers. In time, key concepts in the program would become part of the company's everyday language.

Besides the just-introduced Covey training, both Unilever and UVGN had programs for individual development that involved competency assessments and 360-degree feedback, followed up by skill training. But what was needed to get the workforce oriented and prepared for a future of growth was something bigger, something more encompassing, something they had never done before.

Spotlight: Hans Cornuit

Hans Cornuit had started his career as personnel manager in UVGN and returned ten years later to UVGN to become its HR director. His résumé had a history of factory closures and disposals and, as a colleague put it, he was "rather good in doing these kinds of tough things" and "restructuring companies in a brilliant way." When he arrived, all that mattered was bringing down costs, and the business was being run by an extreme hierarchy and very short time horizon. Hans thought this was no way to run a business, let alone grow it.

The father of three girls, Hans pioneered the people development path of the transformation by introducing Covey's *Seven Habits* training. "To convey the message that it was important," he says, he would personally open every training course, and "to break the ground a bit" he would talk about how difficult it was to raise his youngest daughter, who was extremely clever and beautiful.

"I think over 90 percent of what I am doing is different from what I did five years ago and that's great fun," said Hans. "Bringing numbers down may be satisfying but it is not fun. The fun is in the new elements and looking at change and transformation processes and all the dynamics behind it in fact. The fun is to change mindsets, to no longer work within the same old paradigms."

Getting the Whole Company Involved

In the fields of organization development and change, there was at this time growing interest and expertise in what were termed *whole system interventions* that would bring large numbers of people together in a dialogue about business conditions and develop new outlooks and skills.[3] In addition, the various disciplines of organizational learning were also being refined and gaining a following.[4] Drawing on both these methodologies, UVGN decided to get the whole organization together in what was termed a Learning Conference.

Jeff Pitt, a Covey trainer, was tapped to design and facilitate the event. It would be a new experience for managers and employees to gather together for anything more than a simple presentation. They would have to talk, do things together they had never tried before, and experience the emotions associated with learning something new together. They would not only learn about the current state of the business but also explore the implications of the growth agenda and their responsibilities in it. They would do some group exercises and experience the challenge and fun of learning together rather than as individuals.

All of this would be done under a theme carefully chosen to reaffirm the challenges the company faced, acknowledge the progress already made, and set new—seemingly impossible—targets for the next six months.

"People Make the Difference"

All UVGN employees assembled in February 1996 at Land van Ooit (Once Upon a Time Land), a theme park in Drunen in Holland's province of Brabant (Land of In-Between). They walked to a huge tent, and when they stepped inside, loud rock-and-roll music played as live local entertainers greeted them.

The first company-wide Learning Conference set the tone for what would come to be called UVGN's "new beginning." Everyone together—all the factory people, the sales and marketing people, the office people. Everyone hearing and seeing the numbers. Everyone talking about the business, and about themselves. Everyone dressed casually, even the bosses in jeans, and everyone wearing themed "People Make the Difference" T-shirts!

When their new chairman took the stage to talk about the business, he used bold PowerPoint slides with colorful graphics projected on the giant screen behind him. As the show continued, there were group tasks, more entertainment, a video of highlights of the day. And at the end of the day—a feast and party! It was a mix of showmanship and high-tech infotainment that is still comparatively rare at company conferences. Imagine its impact in southern Holland in 1996. . . .

After getting grounded in the state of the business, people gathered in small groups to draw and discuss the linkages between their personal aspirations and the company's goals. They talked about how they would like to see the business evolve over the next five years and shared their personal expectations and concerns.

This was the first time many of the factory and office workers had ever been exposed to anything like this. Some had difficulty participating in the experiential learning activities, but all in all, most were excited about what was happening and let themselves be cast into new roles. "It really felt like a new beginning," said one plant manager, adding:

> There were results. The atmosphere was positive. We could say look
> at what we have done—you saw costs going down, building in the
> business logic again. . . . We also saw we had to do more things like
> a learning conference.

In the months that followed, the T-shirts handed out at the conference and a video of the day's highlights served as a reminder of the fun and of the promises people had made to one another. And every employee received a plastic card summarizing the key messages of the event: One side showed interconnected pieces of a puzzle with the labels *productivity, quality, innovation*; on the reverse were the company goals they had promised themselves to reach.

A second UVGN Learning Conference held that fall stuck to the same general scheme: lively music at the beginning and end of the day, videos showing some of the things that had happened, presentations in an upbeat style, and managers together with workers in freewheeling small group discussions and eye-opening "experiential learning" activities. In one, participants learned how to juggle! This simple task viscerally demonstrated that everyone could learn new tricks. The broader message was that new capabilities were needed to grow the business. A "flying in formation" exercise underscored the benefits of collective effort.

"The key message," said one of UVGN's engineers, "was if you really want and get professional training and coaching, you can learn much more than you ever think. You can do far more than you think you're capable of." And this time, the plastic wallet cards zeroed in on the long-term perspective and communicated the company's new strategic intent: "2x Growth."

Teams Perform More

Another part of the "new beginning" in 1996 was the Total Preventive Maintenance program—its name eventually morphed into Teams Perform More, or TPM.[5] Sponsored by Unilever, who (along with leading automotive, electronic, and high-tech manufacturers) looked to Japan for best practices to adopt to improve productivity and quality, TPM was viewed within UVGN as yet another way to develop people and build its business.

To launch it, Unilever sent senior manufacturing and quality managers to Japan to learn from TPM specialists at local factories. But at UVGN, with its developing notions of empowerment and people development, sixteen people from all levels, including factory operators and union representatives, visited Japanese companies, and many others went to European factories for benchmarking.

TPM had been announced at the first UVGN Learning Conference in February, and it was kicked off with a training program for four pilot teams in April. Jose Cavanna, from the consulting firm Proudfoot, arrived to teach, coach, and drive progress. By July, as a result of extensive training, workshops, and benchmarking trips to

Japan and around Europe, thirty-six action teams were in place, re-porting improvements and sharing their learning with one another.

The benchmarking trips alone were a stimulating experience. "For all of us, all the operators and technicians," said one plant op-erator, "our eyes were wide open and we kept on asking how we could set it up." What really produced new action, though, were the new ways of thinking that TPM sparked—for workers, supervisors, and managers. As a UVGN plant manager saw it:

> TPM should not be driven by me but driven by the supervisors below me. It is the way to build people so I was constantly driving my supervisors to implement TPM. I tried to enable them to make it possible by giving them training, tools, or the money they needed.

The implementation of TPM was not without its missteps. Some machine operators expected to race ahead to improvement before learning to walk. They espoused the TPM message, but they kept to the old way of doing things and did not master the new ap-proach and its required discipline. Also, efficiency gains varied from line to line. The TPM methodology wasn't oriented toward quick wins. Changing the culture in factories wound up taking time and proceeding in fits and spurts.

What was crucial was that management began to listen to the people. "The people who before '95 only stood there, doing their job and nothing else, now were listened to," said a machine opera-tor. "Their ideas were taken over. If someone had an idea to change something in the machines that cost money, it happened."

Enter the Young Leaders

With a broadly communicated strategic agenda and TPM and Covey training set in motion, the company now needed to gain speed and show gains.

In the early fact-finding and business review phases of the turn-around, Gunning and Synhaeve had bypassed the formal management ranks to look for creative thinking and fresh minds. They put together an informal group of leaders, choosing people who had sharp, analytic minds and an appetite to drive business improvements— and who weren't wedded to the past. Among them were the chief engineer Rein Ettema, the finance director Kees Ekelmans, and the controller Hein Swinkels, as well as some young, talented people from the lower ranks including Mick van Ettinger, Evert Bos, Ad van Oers, Roef van Duin, and Rob Schaerlaeckens. Most of this group had little formal authority to implement changes. They soon encountered management board members who had different ideas about who was in charge.

Frankly, the company's senior managers clearly lacked the mindset and skills needed to support UVGN's new growth agenda. Many of the existing board members had been selected, and promoted, based on their analytical acumen and were groomed in the distant personal style expected of financial managers. And while they had administered the operation effectively in a stable environment, they lacked the business knowledge and ambition to grow the business under current conditions, let alone double performance. They would have to be replaced.

"There was hardly any debate about it," said Hans Cornuit, continuing:

> Everyone could see from the first day onwards what was really going on. The important issue was to pick two or three people high up in the hierarchy and get them out. From one day to the other. Not only because they were not performing well but to make the point that we could do without them. That was very important. We had far too many layers.

It was clear to almost everyone that it was absolutely necessary to make these changes. A plant manager recalled that even one of the ladies from the canteen once spoke out about the number of layers: "There are too many captains on the ship!" she said. "You're absolutely right," Gunning replied, "and we are going to do something about it!" Two weeks later one layer of factory managers was sent home. "That was a very strong statement," the plant manager said, "especially since people lower in the organization felt that they had always been right."

Reaching into the Ranks

To run each of the businesses, Gunning and Synhaeve now reached into the ranks of their young leaders, sometimes deep into the ranks. As before, the people they chose were not the prototypical Unilever high-flyers. These new leaders were close to the action, energetic, business minded, not from top universities but "students of management," hungry to succeed—and sometimes very young. They would be key to setting the new direction and tone of the business.

"The basic approach was we build a new organization," recalls Rein Ettema, the chief engineer, "we build a new management style, laying down the strategy of the company. It was a very young team of managers that was around the table. A very unconventional way." One of them, Roef van Duin, for example, had been with UVGN only three years. He had started as a shift leader in the sauce factory in 1993 and was promoted to production manager in 1995. Now he suddenly had full authority and profit-and-loss accountability for a plant.

The situation was different in marketing and sales than it was in the factories—no promising leaders were within easy reach. "In marketing and sales the chairman had nobody he could depend on," according to a controller. "He had to drill down until he found very young people that he could work with." By skipping levels in the organization to promote new leaders Gunning was betting on potential rather than proven performance. Young people have not had the experience, and you do not really know until you test them if they will have the needed abilities. And how would employees react to the new recruits? Could the young leaders assert authority? What if they couldn't deliver results? "We gambled with many things," said Gunning. "I recall that we appointed Roef, for instance, who was inexperienced at that time and very young as a plant manager. We wanted to do things differently. And we wanted to make the point that we were going to take risks. And when we gave Roef the job he lived up to the expectations."

Unox Takes the Stage

The 1995–1996 restructuring and cost savings had created a ship that didn't require constant bailing and was able to float, if not to plunge ahead immediately. Now with new leaders in place and the savings coming in from layoffs and delayering, new investments could be made. Responsibility was pushed down as the business lines were given profit-and-loss accountability. The stage was set to push for new activities leading to growth.

The Zwan fresh meat factory had been sold around mid-year, and by 1996 year-end, UVGN could show a 25 percent improvement in operational efficiencies and, excluding the sale of the Zwan factory, cost reductions of NLG 48 million overall. All this freed up resources to reinvest in brands. Chicken Tonight, a product aimed at people with busy lives, was relaunched as a "convenient and time saving" treat for families and singles. A relaunch of Unox's wet soups emphasized a broad appeal with their healthy ingredients—and soon the perception of the brand would be completely transformed.

Though the Unox label was well known, it was still seen as a quiet brand, predominantly recognized by housewives looking on grocery store shelves. The beginning of the change of its image would be marked with a well-crafted promotion, aided by a bit of luck and a splash of serendipity.

Part II

Takeover

Chapter 3

Merger or Takeover?

We heard rumors that UVGN would merge with
VdBN and that [Gunning] might succeed our
chairman. . . . We awaited his arrival in fear and
horror.

—*Sales director*

The new year of 1997 arrived with unusually cold weather, freezing
all the canals of Holland—something that happens roughly once
every ten years. The country celebrates this special occurrence with
a spontaneous holiday called *Elfstedentocht*—a skating tour of the
canals that touches eleven cities across the country. Everyone has a
day off, and all who are able to get out on their skates head for the
canals for a day of fun and play. *Elfstedentocht* is the news of the day,
broadcast on national television and covered by all the newspapers.
Tens of thousands of skaters, in towns large and small, are out on
the ice.

Flashback (several months earlier): On a hot summer day in
China, a decision had been made to purchase 500,000 orange knit
hats with the Unox logo on the front. No one had a specific plan in
mind for them, but they were a good buy and looked to be useful
someday. As *Elfstedentocht* dawned, UVGN marketers had a brain-
storm. Soon, they were all out on waterways giving away the orange
hats to passing skaters. Thousands of people wearing knit hats in the
national color of Holland—and sporting the Unox logo—captured
the attention of the entire country that day.

Later, in a further show of enthusiasm, dozens of Unox employees assembled en masse, stripped off virtually everything but their orange hats, and ran for a celebratory plunge into the wintry North Sea.

The Whole Nation Was Watching

"Everybody was wearing the Unox hats we gave out," HR director Cornuit said about the national skate, "and the event was broadcast live on television for fourteen hours or so. It was fantastic! The whole nation was watching." And the Unox brand and the orange hats made it to front page of national newspapers the next morning—the kind of advertising money can't buy.

"We had been trying to find an event which would fit with the Unox brand," recalled an account manager from the company's advertising agency. "Then came *Elfstedentocht*. . . . We gave sausages away and soup on the ice itself. 'Thank You, Unox' was on the headings of all papers. Everybody forgot the dust layers—the image that had previously characterized the brand."

In a rare combination of planning and serendipity, putting the orange Unox hats on a nation of skaters was an inspired product promotion for a brand that was losing share and considered boring. Fixing quality had improved taste and in time improved margins, but substantial market gains required repositioning the product and giving the brand greater appeal.

The skating event associated Unox with fun and energy while enhancing the company's image and its workers' pride in their product and their employer. And the dive into the North Sea was momentous: like a baptismal revival of a company once pronounced dead. It symbolized UVGN's rebirth as an organization ready to face the challenge that came with the new year: merging with another Unilever business and becoming the largest food company in the Netherlands.

The Guy from UVGN

The announcement that the chairman of UVGN would preside over the merger with Van den Bergh Nederland (VdBN) set the grapevine buzzing. "We heard that Mr. Gunning was creating havoc at UVGN," said a VdBN sales director. "And we also heard rumors that UVGN would merge with VdBN and that he might succeed our chairman. The rumor circuit was decidedly negative."

VdBN was the older, larger company and one of the two founding companies that had formed Unilever. It traced some of its history to Anton Jurgens and Simon van den Bergh, the Dutch butter traders and margarine pioneers, competitors since 1870, who joined forces to create the "Margarine Union" in 1927. Shortly afterward the Union had merged with the Lever brothers of England to form Unilever, which named its margarine factory after Van den Bergh and Jurgens.

The other branch of VdBN's family tree traced back to 1884, when J. C. van Marken set up his Dutch oil factory. From peanuts he fabricated edible vegetable oils, which are the most important component for margarine. In 1897, Marken's firm merged with a similar company in Bordeaux led by Emmanuel Calvé. Calvé became the brand name for a range of innovative products, including peanut butter, and set up its operations in a Dutch factory in Delft. In 1991 Van den Bergh & Jurgens merged with Calvé and the combined and renamed company operated under the acronym VdBN.

How Can This Happen?

When the merger with UVGN was announced, VdBN was the major food company in Holland and in the United Kingdom, homes to the corporation's twin international headquarters. The headquarters offices of Unilever's top corporate management in Rotterdam could be seen from VdBN's windows. And marketers from all over Europe flocked to the company known as the "University of

Brands." UVGN was located in the provincial southern part of Holland, well away from the corporate spotlight and surely not a magnet for talent. What would it have to offer to the combination?

Reactions to the merger at VdBN ranged from shock to skepticism to defiance about the prospects for the change. For example:

- *From a quality assurance manager:* "Normally the richer or stronger company takes over in a merger. So the chairman of Van den Bergh should have been the chairman of both companies. In this case, it was the opposite and a big shock to the traditional Margarine Kings. The guy from UVGN becoming chairman had big implications."

- *From a sales director:* "We were caught by surprise and we thought: 'We as big as Van den Bergh are being taken over by that loss-making company UVGN. How can this happen?'"

- *From a marketing manager:* "There was an anxiety and insecurity based on the changes we heard happened in UVGN. Our mindset was, 'We are Van den Bergh. We do not need change because we are invincible.'"

Another New Beginning

Gunning promised a "new beginning" as he took over VdBN. But as one observer put it, "This was a huge shift from 'how are we going to save this business?' to 'how are we going to manage the merger?'" It was a far bigger and more challenging task. Would he really challenge the fundamentals of the business?

The business logic for merging UVGN and VdBN was sound. Combining the two headquarters and staff functions would yield immediate cost savings and bring some economies of scale to the business. The merged company could show a single face to retailers and consolidate its purchasing, advertising, and distribution activities. It would be the largest food business in the Netherlands.

For several months prior to the merge, Marijn van Tiggelen, a finance specialist who had started at corporate and then moved to

UVGN, prepared cost-benefit studies of various integration options for the two companies. Four conclusions were reached:

- There would be two business units—one concerned with spreads and cooking oils, VdBN products made from yellow fats, and the other involving foods, which would join Unox products with several VdBN brands (see Figure 3.1).

- The factories would be organized into sourcing units for Foods and Fats to supply products for one of the two business units to market and sell.

- A small out-of-home culinary business, Uniquisine, would be established to sell products to restaurants and cafeterias.

- Finally, headquarters would be located in Rotterdam and the combined business would be known as Van den Bergh Nederland. Brand names would be kept and used to maintain market identity with consumers.

Figure 3.1 The Merged VdBN Organization Structure

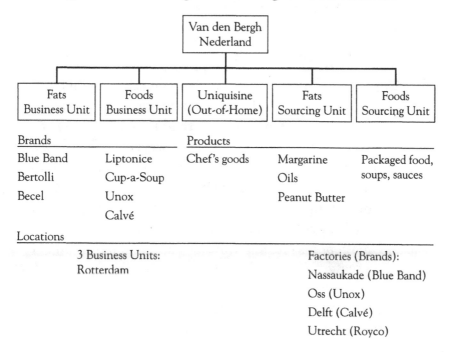

The Fastest Merger You Could Imagine

There were differences of opinion, however, about how fast to proceed on integration. One school of thought was to take "a year or so" to look into the situation, develop plans, and win people over. Gunning made a different choice—to do it quickly, and in one go:

> It was the fastest merger you could imagine. Within sixteen days of the decision it was in operation. We had to move a whole company, sell some offices, and define a new structure. People had to get into place, systems had to be integrated, and trade terms had to be harmonized. Families and houses had to be moved.
>
> Coming from a company that had been in total disarray [UVGN] and going into a long transition would be a killer. That is where the story of the fast merger starts. We formed business units, all profit-and-loss account responsible. In hindsight, a fantastic decision. There were dedicated groups of people in Foods, Fats, and Factories that had to deliver their targets. The merger pain started, but people were clear about their responsibilities and focused in their thinking and action.

No matter the commercial logic, there are psychological factors that work against a merger of equals—even in combinations of units within a firm.[1] Each side in this combination was projected to gain and lose some advantage over the other, and many things would remain unchanged. There was, however, a palpable fear in VdBN that their South Holland counterparts would dominate them. "Gunning said that it should be done in a hundred days," said a VdBN marketing manager. "He took the whole merger on as a personal battle, I don't know why. Maybe it had something to do with his youth or his previous time at VdBN. I'll never forget him basically saying: 'We will show how strong UVGN is and how empty Van den Bergh is.'"

And with the fear came resistance. As a VdBN PR director put it: "We felt we were a great company. We will survive this chairman, let him come here if he likes, but we will continue doing what we always have done. People thought that the guys from UVGN, the amateurs, would learn their lessons when they came to Rotterdam."

A Flawed Entrance

To heighten the natural fears even further, the new chairman made a clumsy and controversial entry into VdBN. The outgoing chairman and his management board had arranged to meet the incoming chairman at the front entrance to VdBN headquarters. Instead, Gunning entered through the Nassaukade factory, located behind the HQ office, and greeted factory workers, some of who were still there from his time on the processing line during college, twenty-five years earlier. Some saw this as a symbol of his affinity for the "common man." A few saw it as "playing to the crowd." In any case, this new "curtain raiser" was a harbinger of further upset.

Next came a series of challenging questions about the health of the business. In several forums, Gunning questioned VdBN's profit and volume projections and expressed concerns about marketing plans. In the months prior to the merger, he had pored over due-diligence data and developed legitimate concerns about the business. But as he first took over, rather than deepening everyone's understanding of the situation, the incoming chairman was perceived as pointing the finger.

"I remember quite well Gunning praising UVGN and saying that everything was working quite well," recalled a sales services manager. "He said it was the opposite at Van den Bergh . . . that the company was asleep." Misapprehension and resistance deepened. "Take the slogan 'a new beginning,'" said one VdBN manufacturing manager, "to me this meant that what you all have now is rubbish. Who says we have to start anew? . . . There was quite some friction."

After his predecessor's farewell party, tensions reached a crescendo. On the day of the event, according to one manager, "Tex refused to follow tradition to shut down the factories for the farewell party. Then, when the party started, he stood there with his arms folded over his chest, observing it all. The expression on his face said it all." When Gunning took the stage, his remarks cast doubts on VdBN's performance and spoiled the festive mood.

The new chairman's opening act, on a new and bigger stage, was a decided flop. More broadly, the criticism that he intended to be a wake-up call failed to register any alarm. As one manager recalled, "We felt alienated because we believed that we *had* changed. Our new leader was basically putting us down."

In hindsight, Gunning acknowledged that his entrance into VdBN was a mistake: "I had been working in this company since I was eighteen years old. I knew it was a good company and appreciated its history. But I also knew it had been losing volume for years and was losing market share. When I saw the exuberant celebration at the party, I panicked. I sensed deep weaknesses—a lack of realism and humbleness. I wanted to challenge the omnipotent attitude."

Culture Clash

Efforts to merge the two companies were also hampered by their different histories, structures, markets, products, geographies, and people. The intellectual, marketing-minded, city-based people at VdBN from northern Holland did not mesh well with the down-to-earth, farm- and factory-oriented UVGN people from southern Holland. These differences were immediately evident in their merger mindsets and management styles—a classic culture clash in the making (see Exhibit 3.1).[2]

For months after the merger, an "us against them" attitude pervaded the newly merged organization. Some from VdBN, for example, clung to their past accomplishments and their feelings of superiority over the farmers from South Holland. "This was a very professional organization," said one account manager. "We had a lot more data than they had at UVGN, a much broader history and people who were far more experienced. [Our former chairman] introduced slogans like 'Let's innovate.' I think that created a very positive environment."

Exhibit 3.1 In Their Own Words: VdBN and UVGN Cultural Differences

VdBN	UVGN
Background . . .	
Location: Rotterdam, close to Unilever HQ	**Location:** Oss, in southern Holland
History: One of the two founding companies of Unilever, from century-old roots	**History:** Heritage in fresh meat business goes back a century
Business: Profitable	**Business:** Loss-making
People: Intellectual, marketing savvy, city-slick	**People:** Down-to-earth, manufacturing, "farmers" and "cowboys"
On Their Merger Mindset . . .	
Marketing manager A: We believed that we were the center of excellence in marketing, especially for margarine, in the world.	**Shift leader:** Where we started from was destruction and threats to close factories. We were against the wall. We wanted to survive and there was a clear need to change.
On Management Style . . .	
Sales director: It was a very hierarchical organization. With the customers everything was always going "fantastic" but nobody wanted to see them inside the gate. You had targets, but they did not really care whether you achieved them or not.	**General manager Foods (former):** UVGN people were used to working in small teams. Everything they did was open to questioning.
General manager Foods (former): Van den Bergh was very well organized, like a ministry of marketing. Lots of procedures, lots of people, and so on.	**Distribution manager:** At UVGN everything was a lot looser. People felt more comfortable and were happier. They were not that obstructed by procedures and could therefore be more creative.
Sales director: We were used to top down. You were not even allowed to join the discussion. Somebody else decided for you what your company looked like. You were not allowed a voice in the decision.	**General manager Foods (former):** I would describe UVGN when I arrived as a saloon, or a Wild West town, with a new sheriff. They finally were liberated by a top manager who was directly in contact with them, directly working with the floor, and putting a lot of energy and effort into it.

Others welcomed the change. The new candor in discussions and growing sense of reality about business conditions seemed refreshing. The former general manager of the Fats unit recalled: "The biggest problem that I had with the [old VdBN] culture was that it was very false. A lot of celebration of so-called successes. There was an emphasis on teamwork, but it was not real teamwork. It was more like, 'Let's slap each other on the back, say how fantastic we are doing.' It avoided the real views on what was happening."

The challenge would be for the merged companies to develop a shared view of reality and a vision for going forward. This would mean turning attention away from one another and pointing it toward the marketplace, competitors, and consumer needs. The new chairman would have to teach managers at VdBN, as he had at UVGN, more about the fundamentals of the business. In short, the combined company—now operating under the VdBN name—would have to "go into therapy."

Chapter 4

Going into Therapy

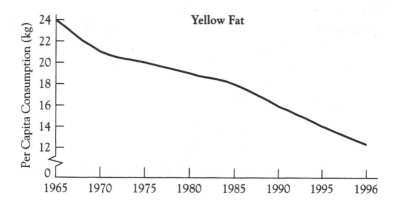

The analogy of "going into therapy" was intentional. For organizations, as for individuals, the aim of psychotherapy is to develop a clear, "reality-based" picture of yourself and your circumstances.[1] It started at VdBN with a period of digging into facts and figures, particularly about the state of the yellow fats business.

All of a sudden a mirror was held up to a company where everybody thought, "We are fantastic!" And it showed that things were horribly wrong. The new leaders coming in from UVGN could much more easily see the need for change than could those who had congratulated themselves for decades on their success.

"The most revealing thing was a simple graph," said the HR director (referring to the one pictured at the start of this chapter). "It showed what was happening with our volume. Simply looking at the figures showed how you had to keep increasing the price to make quarterly or yearly results. It opened up reality."

Wake-Up Call II

For twenty years the margarine market had been in decline. And for twenty years, VdBN had maintained its income by raising prices and closely managing its raw material costs. In that sense the situation was a replica of the UVGN case, so the same intellectual arguments could be used to convince people that they had to do something. But UVGN had been a loss-making business for years and was facing bankruptcy when Hans and Tex entered the scene. A sense of urgency was there. Not so with VdBN. They were making huge amounts of money year after year, and they were seen as very successful.

Another wake-up call was needed, something that would galvanize the company the way the tour of the warehouse of waste had roused UVGN. This time, the approach would be less visceral and emotional and more analytical. As Gunning recalled it:

> In any business, there is always, somewhere and somehow, an insight that signals a compelling need for change. Once you have found that insight, you can use symbols, like for instance a graph showing future problems, to make the need for analysis and change tangible. You can find something in every company that goes wrong and help people to accept the consequences and to voluntarily accept that they should go into analysis. At VdBN, it was the per capita consumption of margarine, which had been in decline for years, that got us into analysis.

Bringing in strategy consultants helped to prepare the intellectual ground. At first there was a lot of resistance; managers were convinced there was no need for outside help until they saw all the results. "Some of the barriers to change were perceptual," said one of the consultants. "People were just not aware of what was really going on inside the business. Still others were just not deeply steeped enough in business, let alone in their own business."

Vulnerable Volume

VdBN managers began to see how they had achieved past profit targets because they could increase prices in the face of declining sales volumes. But the margarine market as a whole was in decline (see Table 4.1). And competition for market share was growing more intense. Raising their awareness of these competitive dynamics helped to create a sense of crisis for VdBN managers. "Vulnerable volume" was the phrase that denoted the need for change.[2]

As Neil Wickers, then general manager of Fats, put it:

> The first step was to set up the current reality of what was happening to our business. We went into it thinking that our market share was stable and actually discovered that it had been declining for the past four years. We went into it thinking that our profits were increasing because we had been reducing costs and found that our profits had only been increasing because we had raised prices.
>
> This created a sense of urgency—not that we are on the edge of the cliff, but the sense of urgency that we have to do something now or otherwise we will be on the edge of a cliff.

Fats Fight for Share

The decline in the Fats unit's volume was having a significant impact on profitability—one that would only get worse over time. The unit's leaders realized that fighting for share as the overall market

Table 4.1 P&L Trends in Yellow Fats

	1993	1994	1995	1996
Volume Sold Fats (in tons)	123	116	112	112
Impact of Volume Loss on Fats P&L (annual %)	−10.4	−21.1	−27.3	−27.1

declined would require a rigorous look into prevailing strategies and operations.

When they started their strategic review, a lot of people in Fats were quite skeptical. It was a huge effort. "We spent a lot of time at the office," quipped a marketing manager. But, as soon as the managers started working with the strategy consultants, they began to see the advantages of the process. "A lot of complacent, arrogant managers really started to doubt whether we were doing the right things," said one Fats employee.

The next question was what should be done with the business to make the right shift? After two months of data collection, analysis, and reflection, the brand managers developed proposals. They were asked, for each of the various brands, to propose how to retain or grow market share and profitability. Piece by piece a picture of the overall business took shape. It was an intellectual exercise, because, as one manager put it, "there was no inspiration," and, as another said, "there were too many arguments why it was totally impossible to turn around the overall market decline."

Foods Seeking Growth

The Foods business unit had grown, but only modestly in the years prior to the merger (Table 4.2). The melding of VdBN and UVGN product lines gave the combined unit some administrative and operating synergies but no discernable new opportunities for growth. The new management team would also have to look carefully at their business.

The Foods team had inherited the existing UVGN Strategic Programme 2002, which they adapted to the combined portfolio of the new company. For soups, there would be an initiative to achieve

Table 4.2 Sales Growth in Foods

	1993	1994	1995	1996
Volume Sold Foods (in tons)	108	109	112	116

"scratch quality." The goal was to have their product equal the quality of dishes made from scratch—something that would appeal to the growing number of households with both spouses working. A proposed line of instant noodles would introduce an Asian snack food into Holland, targeted at young adults and students—market segments that the team's research had shown to be ripe for foods associated with creative experimentation and exotic novelty. Other areas of focus included developing products and promotions aimed at the growing snack and out-of-home market segments.

It all looked fine on paper, but the problem—apparent from the start—was that the Foods group managers could not agree on their growth agenda. What's more, they were not organized to market and sell new products through new channels. The strategic program had shown some new directions but had not addressed the organizational changes needed to accomplish them.

The Psychology Game

The intellectual nature of the wake-up call in VdBN was a stark contrast to the visceral, emotional scene in the UVGN warehouse of waste. Still, many of the techniques used in the UVGN turnaround proved useful. Informal conversations, small group workshops, and the strategic review process were used to broaden understanding of the current reality and mobilize support for action. This was aimed not just at VdBN but also at the corporate headquarters. Any changes in strategy—and signs of resistance—would be visible to Unilever's top executives.

It was a brilliant approach, as Aart-Jan (AJ) van Triest, the Fats marketing director, observed:

> It was the psychology game. By letting the group depict their own current reality and the outlook of that reality and then asking the question, "Is this what you want?" And then they fall into the trap of saying, "No, this is not what we want." OK, if that is not what you want, let's change it. It sounds simple, but it is difficult to achieve.

We came from a quite arrogant, rich, static company. It took us a while to warm up. To shake the muscles, start moving and change some of what we believed in seriously. . . .

It takes a lot of effort and intellectual power to let a group who is successful and who think they are doing the right thing come to the conclusion that it is not right. This changed the mental maps of people.

Changing Mindsets

The new chairman's hands-on style also helped to win some people over. Again and again, he met with small groups to mobilize support and move them to action. In so doing, a new tone was set in the company. "There was a very different way of working with the people in terms of mind mingling," observed a Unilever senior VP. "There was a very substantial shift, from a company with a university mindset to one which said, 'Let's do it. Let's get on with it, let's move into action.'"

All kinds of new ideas started coming into the company. A new vocabulary was swiftly introduced. "What was convincing about the new chairman's story was that he had a business language," recalled a VdBN brand manager. "That impressed us. 'Listen to this guy with all this new business talk.'"

Suddenly there were all kinds of groups meeting with each other. People at all levels mobilized themselves. The rapid pace of activity and change left little time for people to reminisce about the past. "It was a kind of fixing things on the run," recalled Neil Wickers, "and everybody working fifteen to twenty hours a day to really make the integration happen in such a short time period. So there were not the structured meetings as I was used to, it was more ad hoc."

But a new culture does not emerge overnight, no matter how strong the leadership or business case for it. Part of culture change depends on the relationships that are developed as people work together face-to-face, creating a new group that thinks and acts differently, one that people want to be a part of and want to be identified with. By midyear 1997, the need to change was widely understood, but differences remained in terms of how people saw each other and what they were willing to do. Former UVGN people would have to work in a more structured and professional way. Former VdBN people were moving into a very aggressive change culture.

Finding small activities and projects to get people working together helped build the skills and attitudes needed for addressing the larger business issues together. Recalled Hans Cornuit, the HR director:

> I remember meeting with all the VdBN HR people. Half of them were thinking, "These guys are farmers from the south of Holland." It took quite some time to get them on board. In the end what worked extremely well was to find projects where we had common goals and work together on those. Organizing the first Learning Conference at VdBN was such a project. People picked up on the fun in organizing these events and mobilizing others.

Competing for the Future

In March 1997, the two thousand employees of the postmerger VdBN gather in a theater in Den Haag (The Hague) to attend the inaugural Learning Conference of the merged organization. The event is a new-generation learning conference—everything, it seems, has been taken to the next level of engagement and showmanship. The thinking behind the staging and activities now is that they must be both "intellectually convincing and emotionally appealing"—one of many new ideas coming into the company's mindset and everyday vocabulary.[3] To relaunch and brand the practice of bringing the whole company together for a day of learning, there is a new conference logo featuring *Star Trek*-like figures to capture the essence of the company's new challenge: "Competing for the Future."

The day begins with a detailed review of the current business situation, presented via slides on a large screen, with eye-catching graphs, pithy summaries, and thought-provoking conclusions. Besides the picture of current performance, business outlook, and plans for 1997 for each of the business and sourcing units, the presentations hammer home the message about "vulnerable volume." Then the spotlight turns to poor operating efficiencies in the factories.

It is already a mind-opening experience for both VdBN staff and factory workers, most of whom have never been exposed to an event like this, much less this kind of business results information or having their chairman share what he is thinking. At the end of the presentations, there is one question on everyone's mind: What is to be done?

Gunning answers it with a dramatic move: Grabbing the mike and stepping back from the podium, he announces, "I cannot do it for you! You have to do it yourselves. The future is in your hands." A buzz goes through the theater and continues through the morning's work unit discussions and into lunch. "It was very intense—a bowl of energy," said one of the shift leaders who was at the conference. "We talked about ourselves in business, about the power we have in our own hands. We have to go for our own future; we compete for the future of our business."

The afternoon's activities are empowerment and teaming games—a new way of learning in Holland and certainly novel for office and factory workers. They are organized into over a hundred small groups and challenged to think "out of the box" as the games begin.

At one point, for instance, the notion of taking responsibility was illustrated through a martial arts exercise. Facilitators demonstrated how to do what appeared to be the impossible—to break a wooden board in two with a karate punch. It looked hard, but with concentration and courage it could be done. As board after board cracked apart throughout the theater, the point was made loud and clear. Another exercise demonstrated how people can do bold things with the support of others. In "trust falls," people were asked to fall backward off a table into the arms of their teammates. The experience brought abstract notions of teamwork and interdependence to life.

There was some initial resistance, then most of the participants quickly warmed to their tasks. "At first I thought, 'What kind of nonsense is this?'" said one participant. "I wondered how this could be of any use. But I had never heard people talking so clearly about very complex issues in such a relaxed manner." Subsequent discussions about applying the lessons back on the job were fruitful. "People spoke about their own practice, not from the book, but from their own experience. For me that is gold," said another.

The first VdBN-wide Learning Conference ended with a show of solidarity—everyone standing together, each holding a candle. Two thousand points of light conveyed the idea that each person made a difference—and all were needed for VdBN to compete for the future.

More Highly Effective People

The 1997 Learning Conference also introduced into VdBN the *Seven Habits* principles already familiar to the UVGN contingent. Now the Covey courses would be expanded throughout the company as Hans van't Sant, a line manager, took charge of the training and launched a train-the-trainers program at VdBN with Covey representative David Saunders.

As participation in the training spread, its impact was increasingly significant. "In the course of two, three days we could usually get the crap out and get to high levels of involvement," said Saunders. "A lot of people translated the content into what they were doing within their own group." Phrases like "circle of influence," "emotional bank account," and "sharpen your saw"—all popularized in *Seven Habits*—became a part of VdBN's everyday language. In the words of one participant, "It enabled us to say to each other, 'Hang on a minute, stop thinking in terms of constraints, be proactive,' without people being offended."

All in all, the Covey training began to deepen people's understanding of human behavior and enabled them to think and talk about their relationships at work. "We knew implicitly all that we talked about," said one production manager, "but it was handy to make it explicit, put it all out, and see the relationships between ideas. It opened my eyes."

Index 100

Through that spring, the Fats team had been on a mental and emotional roller coaster—from skepticism to appreciating the value of the strategic review, from refusing to acknowledge the trouble the business faced to eventual acceptance of the significance of "vulnerable volume." As their denial died out, depression took hold—they couldn't see their way forward. As van Triest, the Fats marketing manager, put it: "Tex didn't have an answer. He didn't know how to grow volume. We were on our own."

About midyear, the hands-on involvement in studying the situation in Fats began to pay off. That was when Neil Wickers and van Triest hit upon an idea. They set a stretch goal, naming it Index 100, and declared that "not one more percentage of volume would be lost."[4]

It was an inspired move. Setting stretch goals injects uncertainty and energy into a business. This type of goal is one that you cannot achieve with existing knowledge and practices. You have to invent something new. "We quickly discovered that we don't know the answers," Wickers recalled.

> With stretch targets, we agreed that we do not know how to do that and that no one had ever done it before. Therefore, the only way that we will actually achieve these stretch targets is by working together and inventing new ways of doing things.

Index 100 worked intellectually—but also emotionally. It was the first time that Fats had a team target. Previously people said, "I want a separate target for my brand because I can only influence what *my* brand does." Index 100 was about people working together.

"When you say in a declining market we have to achieve Index 100," said a Fats buying director, "that's a very ambitious way of growing your market share. You have to fight your competitors. We rejoiced when hundreds of managers were shouting that Index 100 was the most important thing to achieve. They were so keen in getting it done."

Index 100 unleashed a flurry of creativity in the Fats business. Leon Schoofs, the sales director, said it brought a "new spirit into the organization." His team tracked competitors and fought for share with surgical price reductions and product promotions. Wickers and van Triest focused on the branded portfolio and deemphasized or eliminated some lower-volume brands. Other leaders complemented their efforts by cutting costs, improving relationships with retailers, and finding other ways to make improvements.

"Angry Young Men"

About the same time, in mid-1997, VdBN set up an organizational review team. Just as he had done at UVGN, instead of working with the internal management board, Gunning assembled a team of hand-picked young leaders, including Marijn van Tiggelen and Mick van Ettinger, formerly with UVGN, and AJ van Triest and Kees Kruythoff from Fats.

VdBN had lost 70 million guilders in seven years on "investments on innovation"—product ideas ready for the market that were never launched properly. "Our innovation track record was lousy," said one account manager. "We said, 'Something is wrong.'" And by thinking and taking a closer look, the review team soon found the root of the problem: Brand people were much too busy with operations, so much that they didn't have enough time for the long-term, deep-scale, branded consumer stuff. "They were like little 'general managers,'" said one observer, "deciding everything. They had forgotten the long-term business."

The organizational review team recommended dividing the business units into separate value creation (pure marketing) and value delivery (sales and distribution) functions. The value creation people—the long-term thinkers, the "artists" in the new structure—would be specialists who were to keep the consumer uppermost in mind and focus on development of brand innovations. The value delivery function was likened to a well-oiled machine, focused on annual performance targets. It would consist of the sales force and market planners who were to manage products in distinct foods and fats categories (see Exhibit 4.1).

"The metaphor we used was the Gulf War," said a marketing director on the team. "Schwarzkopf would never have been able to move as fast into Baghdad if he had not had huge weapons to pave the way. So you need people to develop weapons and you need people to fight in the terrain. The skills and competencies of these people are different."

Exhibit 4.1 In Their Own Words: Value Creation Versus Value Delivery

Value Creation	Value Delivery
"They are the people who think long term. People who really get into the consumer, really know the consumer. Not who say they know it, but who really know it."	"This is like an oiled machine. This is a machine focused on year targets. It just operates and gets the results."
"They are artists. And we said, like great painters they should have maybe one student whom they teach the art of, in our case, brand management, consumer understanding, and that kind of stuff."	"Part of it is sales, but value delivery also consists of category management. So delivery is both brand and consumer oriented. And they are the people who connect the brand thinking with the customer thinking, and start thinking it from a category perspective."
"And so, we said: Don't make them managers. Don't make eight people report to them."	

The proposed separation of value creation and delivery still had its problems. Mainly, it overloaded account managers with responsibilities to manage both customers and product categories. So, the team recommended a threesome to run the business. The addition of a commercial director, acting as the "linking pin," would integrate the efforts of the value creation and value delivery directors. But then there would be no clear role for a general manager. Ettinger recalled, "We left a management board member without a job, because we concluded that you don't need a GM. It's much better to have two or three people leading the organization."

The idea was radical. Nowhere in Unilever was there this sort of group, which VdBN people called the "troika"—rather than a single general manager—running a business unit. To many people in the Foods business it seemed that the impetus for the proposed structure came from the UVGN "young leaders"—they were to be the main beneficiaries of the new structure. The proposed positions closely fit their talents and desired working style, and they wouldn't report to a general manager but directly to the company chairman.

Naturally, there was intense resistance from those who stood to lose the most. The discussions grew more heated in the Foods unit through the summer of 1997. Some members of the review team—those pressing hardest to change the leadership structure in Foods—were dubbed the "angry young men."

Chapter 5

Revolution and Chaos

You can call them "the angry young men." They
had an agenda to carry forward and did it despite
the reactions and the resistance they encountered.

—*PR director*

Conflict had been brewing between the "angry young men" in the
Foods group and their general manager (GM) since the merger. The
conflict concerned more than personalities: it was a battle of
the new ways taking on the old ways. It exemplified the "us against
them" rivalries between the young UVGN "cowboys" and the more
traditional VdBN managers.[1]

Role conflicts had been identified by the organizational review
as a problem area, and the review team had questioned whether the
Foods business unit needed a general manager at all. Meanwhile,
there were mounting struggles over control of the business—
particularly when it came to repositioning brands for growth and
greater profitability.

For example, even as brand managers sought to extend Cup-a-
Soup products to the youth and student market, advertising place-
ments "aimed at fifty-year-olds" undermined their campaigns. The
overt nature of the conflict and struggle for direction was a "very
visible mistake," according to one manager, and caused some to lose
confidence in their general manager. "What struck me most in the
Foods Group," said a sales service manager, "was that there was no
trust between people, no honesty, and different agendas. In that period it was about power and chaos."

The Revolution in Foods

In the summer of 1997, the GM left for several weeks on his honeymoon. His direct reports—including two "angry young men" seeking greater autonomy and responsibility—sent a letter to the management board demanding that the GM be removed. Gunning met with the GM immediately after he returned from the honeymoon and brought in a group of psychologists who worked with Unilever management to mediate the dispute.

Over the course of several meetings the Foods management team worked to sort through their differences. "It was a hell of a fight," said one participant, "among some pretty pissed-off people." "It was a mutiny," said another. "The group said, 'We have affection for you and respect for you as a person, but we find ourselves unable to move forward with you as our leader.'" One of the psychologists commented, "Nothing in business teaches you how to react in this situation, but the GM did remarkably well maintaining his composure." Still, there was no "win-win solution" that would keep everyone on board.

The denouement, reached in fall 1997, was that the GM was reassigned to another Unilever company. Soon, a troika of young leaders took charge of the Foods business. Hans Mikkelsen remained the sales director (responsible for value delivery), Bauke Rouwers was appointed to head marketing (responsible for value creation), and Marijn van Tiggelen (see spotlight) was named to the new position of commercial director.

Many pointed to the revolution in the Foods group, and the subsequent reorganization, as a breakthrough. It was a revolution because those at lower levels appeared to orchestrate changes at higher levels. That this new organizational structure was created is part of the story, and how the issues were handled and changes were made is another part.

Each person involved had his own story to tell. Where the participants stood and how the revolution affected them colored how they saw the changes. It was like the Japanese film classic

Roshomon—which tells a tale of crime and examines the vagaries of truth by showing the same scene over and over, each time from the viewpoint of a different participant or witness (Exhibit 5.1).

The leadership changes that followed the revolution also were seen differently by different people who participated or observed them from the outside. By some accounts, the changeover was a matter of getting leaders in place who could drive the business. In others, it was pure power politics, a further sign of takeover of the business unit by UVGN.

One marketing manager thought it was a question of cultural values—"whether you want people to manage their careers or you want them to manage the business." As he saw it, "One of the problems in Unilever was that people were busy managing their careers, not the business. There was very little risk-taking here, a lot of people

---

Spotlight: Marijn van Tiggelen

Marijn joined Unilever in 1991, starting in the audit department where he gained a good overview of Unilever. He then went to the research laboratories as a management accountant. In January 1996 he was transferred to UVGN, where he was involved in the restructuring of the site with Tex and Hans, first supporting departments like marketing, then working on a new IT system that would facilitate the integration of UVGN and VdBN.

Gunning then asked him to become his personal assistant to help in the merger of VdBN and UVGN. He became the controller of the Foods business in VdBN following the merger, then one of three to lead the Foods business.

"No one will challenge or question whether Marijn van Tiggelen is a great leader," said Hans Cornuit, the HR director. "While some are simply following Tex, others have the guts to confront him. Marijn is an example of that. He is prepared to have the debate with him. I think that chemistry is extremely important for this company."

Exhibit 5.1   A Multisided Tale:
The Revolution in Foods

The Chairman's Perspective	The GM's Story
Strong and experienced leadership is an essential ingredient for a highly effective team. It was clear that the Foods group had a leadership problem and was not functioning properly.	In hindsight, I think he [Tex] really needed somebody to help him drive the process of change management in the way he wanted to do it.
A successful young high-flyer was appointed to a very senior position. But he was not ready for the tasks at hand. The merging of two cultures and the growth agenda turned out to be too complex given the experience he brought to the team. We took a risk and failed.	My relationship with some key team members changed over time. I had a real trusting and a good relationship with some of them. With others I had a non-trusting relationship. That had been a difficulty from the start. In hindsight, it could be explained by two reasons.
When [GM] came back from his honeymoon, I met with him and advised him to talk it out with his people. We got psychologists in to help. After long discussions and tough times, we went for a win-win, and he got a good job within Unilever. Now he's doing an excellent job in our Home and Personal Care division.	First, they believed I was their savior, and should get solutions to the uncertainty they'd been exposed to. And I couldn't at the time. And, second, there was the trust thing between the chairman and me that didn't really help in my relationship with my team.
This story is important because thereafter, the Foods business went through the roof. Marijn got some space, Bauke was promoted to marketing director, and the team just fell into place.	I had two teams, in a way, one from UVGN and one from VdBN. They weren't trusting of each other. And that got out of control. Maybe some were looking for a different kind of leadership. And maybe they were ready to play more of a leadership role themselves.

Exhibit 5.1 A Multisided Tale:
The Revolution in Foods, Cont'd.

A Consultant's Point of View	Some "Angry Young Men"
The chairman was earnestly committed to do everything that was needed to make [GM] successful. In retrospect nothing could be done to transform him into the podium-type leader that the Foods group needed.	#1: [GM] lacked the experience to give thought leadership to the team. There were smart people on the team. Rather than to accept and build on that experience, he started to do things on his own.
The Foods management group was very skeptical that anything could be done to make the group work well under [GM]'s leadership. We had interviews and found he was isolated. We discovered that the team had withheld business information from him. And I remember when I asked "do you realize the seriousness of what you've been doing?" the group said, "Yes, we do." They were willing to live with the consequences of their actions.	#2: [GM] wasn't aware of his weaknesses and nobody told him about them. Guys lost confidence in him as our leader.
	#3: As conflict became obvious, it was not dealt with head-on and so it accumulated. We spent three days in a hotel with help from consultants who were pretty good in sorting out organizational conflict. Four out of the ten adult males ended up in tears, never wanting to go through anything like this again.
This was basically an unworkable situation and steps were taken to find the right role for [GM] elsewhere within Unilever.	

were just interested in moving up." The view from one of the consultants was, "The team in fact played the very best it could, given the hand we'd been dealt. The team had to confront its fundamental structure and composition."

In the end, even the GM acknowledged that, even though it had not been done "in a proper way," it was better for everybody to change the leadership, to change the structure: "The fact that it happened was not a bad thing for the organization."

A Turning Point

These organizational changes had some fallout: rumbling about "disciples" forming around the chairman and references to his "clones" began to be heard. Even so, the trio leading the foods group moved forward with business improvement efforts for the unit. Not only did the business start to develop, so did the organization and interdependencies among marketing and sales. "The Bauke-Hans-Marijn troika really worked," said one marketing manager, "because they were not in competition with each other. They focused on their core activities and responsibilities and they did not interfere with each other. When that happens, you get loads of space all of a sudden."

The change was a turning point for Foods. Real growth began to pop up. Clear responsibilities were introduced. "Responsibilities went down to people who could make an impact. They got the room and power to drive the business as they wished," said one plant manager. The leadership of the "angry young men" grew to be more widely accepted too. For example, "Marijn was the first finance person who was prepared to think with sales and to reinvest extra money in the market," according to one of the marketing managers he worked with. "That man brought a new dimension into Foods. He was driven. He was involved in both cost and sales."

The hard-won changes bonded the troika as a team that would work together well. Though the result for 1997 was a very modest volume growth of only 1.5 percent overall, the revolution in Foods also sent a signal: sacred cows were not exempt from slaughter under the new regime.

Regrouping and Reconnection

Even though the business was on the uptick, and the Covey seminars were reaching more and more people throughout the company, life was unsettled as 1997 reached its end. The management board, on edge with the shake-up in the Foods unit, felt at risk of being eclipsed by young leaders. "It became more and more apparent that we were sort of running the company," said one of the young leaders. "The board was no longer the only entity in charge."

The aspiration for growth had spread but not yet produced results. Some young marketers, frustrated by the lack of progress, frazzled by the pace, and stressed by the ever-increasing pressure, began to lose enthusiasm. Said one, "You see people destroying their own personal lives to fight the competition. If our leadership is not giving enough space to speed things up it is difficult to get it going. It costs so much personal energy to do that. People say, sorry, I won't do it. My life is worth to me a lot and I am not going to destroy it for a company that is not willing to move."

The decision in Foods had been the right one, but all the expected effects of disrupting a human community began to surface. Some of the old VdBN contingent still asked, Who *are* these farmers from the South? And many in Oss, from the old UVGN ranks of the company, accustomed to their limelight, were feeling left out of the action in Rotterdam. And people from both camps were watching: Were the angry young men in Foods going to take over the whole company?

The year of the merger had clearly meant "out with the old, in with the new." With an eye to the question uppermost in everybody's mind—So, what *is* the new? And does it have a heart and soul?—the chairman and his event team began to plan for a management conference that would reconnect people. "This company had been through a difficult year," recalled Gunning. "That came partly from the speed of the merger. To deal with structural issues, we had done a major organizational review. That was a very critical intervention but it was not enough. We needed to reconnect with who we are, who we want to be, and to the best we have in us."

Gerard Prins, the e-commerce manager who had helped stage the company-wide 1997 Learning Conference, was now given broader license to produce the management event. He and his team worked day and night arranging the venue and bringing in theatrical lighting, a sophisticated sound system, and dramatic visual effects. The staging of this event—as in the UVGN warehouse and in the learning conferences—was aimed, according to Prins (see spotlight), at "taking people to a higher level."

"This was a whole different ballgame," said a graphic artist working with Prins on the event. "How to grab people? How to get them and keep them interested? How to move people through different emotions? And then how to get them back into working mode reality."

Spotlight: Gerard Prins

Gerard Prins was an IT specialist at VdBN, always pushing new ideas into execution, always looking for the new technology. He took it very seriously when he was told that if he had a great idea, he had to "go for it." "I got space and also the environment and the money to do it. Everybody on my team was feeling that everything was possible," Gerard said. He initiated several innovative projects that would eventually win him the award of the e-commerce manager of the year.

"I changed a lot personally when I was asked to create and organize events like the Antwerp management conferences and the learning conferences," said Gerard. "I was asked to do things I'd never done. They were out of the box and there were no boundaries. So if I had to break down a wall, I would do it even if I had to build it up later. I felt this drive and this belief in change. Sometimes I thought that's impossible. I can't do that, but always I said, 'I'll handle that,' and I did. That was fun. Great fun.

"The bad part of the story was that some of my bosses were complaining about the time that I put in on company events. While people said, 'Well done!' about the events, they also said: 'Well, how about the other projects?'"

Antwerp, December 1997

The scene of the December 1997 management conference was a huge hall, in a churchlike building in Antwerp. As they entered the hall, the hundred or so leaders from Foods, Fats, and the factories encountered a massive image that seemed to float above the dimly lit stage. It was a scene from the ceiling of the Sistine Chapel— God's hand reaching out to give life to Adam. The symbolism was spellbinding. People are not alone; they are connected to the divine and to one another.

The chairman took the stage first thing in the morning to review the state of the business. "I put up a mirror to the organization in a way that also encouraged and gave credit to those who deserved it," he recalled. "But it is also my role to say when things are not going well, even if it is my own performance. I was honest and told it straight."

After lunch the managers viewed a clip from the movie *The Abyss*, in which the main characters must choose who will be the one to escape from a leaking submersible and swim to safety to a ship at the surface. As Prins recalled it:

> They have only one oxygen mask. The man gets the mask because he is a better swimmer. He has to drown his wife (though the water is so cold that she has a slim chance to survive the swim to the surface). Once on the ship, she is declared clinically dead. He does not give up until they revive her.

The scene from *The Abyss* was a showstopper. "We had been looking for a piece to get people emotionally involved," said one of the event planners. "It is very hard to find what you need because it has to feel real and very often a lot of films look staged and acted. [This] one is extremely powerful when you haven't seen it before."

After watching this very emotional scene, some of the management board members were crying. While they were in their emotional state, Gunning asked: "Do you feel that there is more in you than just brains, that you also have emotions?" Then, he recalled:

> I told them that I had had a lousy year, both businesswise and personally. It was the first time ever I had been unable to bring a real team together. It frustrated me and kept me off balance. And I therefore had not delivered as a business leader. I apologized.
>
> Then I told them that if we wanted growth we had to connect with each other at a deeper level. That was where we started to discuss emotions. The effect was tangible.

Everyone present had had a lousy year too. The old company culture and establishing ways of doing things were in wreckage. Deeply scarred by its revolution, the Foods group was literally in therapy. *The Abyss* crystallized all their feelings of frustration and distress—there was no love in VdBN, much less the will to sacrifice anything for it.

The managers recognized that they hadn't emotionally connected with one another and that they were not yet a real team. Now they began to talk about how much they cared about the business and what they meant to each other. "We hit a nerve," said a planner, "it appealed to what everyone wanted, and unlocked the energy for growth."[2] The leadership from Foods, Fats, and the factories had lived through their abyss. Now, how could this new spirit spread to the entire organization?

Part III

Transforming the Organization

Chapter 6

180 Leaders in Charge

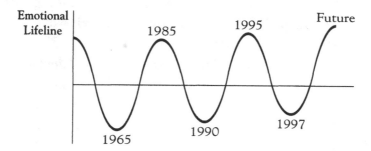

Up to its meeting in Antwerp at the close of 1997, the merged management board had been a lifeless bunch, and each of the business units was starting to go its own way. It was clear that a new orientation was needed if targets for growth were to be accomplished. The closer and deeper relationships that started to form at the management conference in Antwerp would have to permeate the company.

"If you want growth, you need a certain culture," the chairman was fond of saying. "That culture is the same for everybody, requiring real openness and respect. As a leader, to make that happen, you have to be open to others first. Still, it took us awhile to make the link between opening up our emotional side and growing the business."

The challenge for the company's leadership would be to harness the energy that had been unlocked at the Antwerp management meeting and lead VdBN into a new era of growth. At the center of that challenge was the view that deeper levels of openness, engagement, and teamwork among people were crucial for growth and success.

Reconnecting Through Teamwork

"Reconnecting with People" was declared the theme for the 1998 team leader retreat to be held in late February and the company-wide Learning Conference scheduled for March. What could be done there to begin to diffuse through the company what had happened at the Antwerp meeting? And how could it be done with two thousand people? Over the Christmas holidays, as one of the event organizers recalled, "We thought, 'My God, what are we going to do at the Learning Conference? We have to do something with this "Reconnecting with People," but how do we do it with two thousand people? How do we start building a community?'"

The road taken to reconnect VdBN people and develop a community of leaders was influenced by M. Scott Peck's book *The Different Drum*—a favorite of Gunning's that had become popular among VdBN leaders.[1] After a VdBN staffer contacted Peck's nonprofit Foundation for Community Encouragement (FCE) for assistance, Philip Mirvis, then cochair of the FCE Board and visiting professor at the London Business School, met with Gunning and the event-planning team in January 1998.

Gunning, an event planner, and in-house Covey trainer Hans van't Sant wanted something similar to the *Seven Habits* training. An argument erupted over this "cookbook" approach to building community:

> By the time it was two o'clock I was fed up and I started passing notes to a colleague saying, "Look, this guy is just asking questions rather than giving me answers!" She passed a note saying, "This guy is testing you out!" We put that on the table and asked him what he wanted.
>
> We then talked about the issues, where I was in my personal development and where the organization was. We went through a few painful sessions where Phil hammered the fact that it is not about cookbooks. . . .

We came from the angle that you cannot run a business and hold hands and do what you do with community-building circles. People will run away screaming saying this is "Bhagwan" (in reference to the spiritual leader and his cult followers). After some difficulties, we settled on something and started to prepare.

The planning team decided that to reduce any "cultish" connotations and ensure its relevance to businesspeople, the theme of the team leader retreat and the March Learning Conference would be "teamwork" rather than "community building." They looked for thematic consistency with the "highly effective people" language and settled on the idea of building "highly effective teams," or as they were later dubbed, "Top Teams."

Also, they wanted to explore taking team building into an outdoors experience à la Outward Bound–type programs. Partly because Mirvis had long experience with these types of programs, and partly because hiking, biking, and being in nature is part of Dutch culture, the event planners now thought they might include opportunities for the team leaders to make more meaningful connections to nature and to one another in a stimulating outdoor environment.

Some thought the taking-it-outdoors idea was too American, or too much like what other companies in Europe were doing. Then the conceptual breakthrough: VdBN had already embraced the idea of appealing to head *and* heart, why not also soul and body? FCE was bringing in the soul part, and the planning team had learned of a Dutch outdoor training business recently formed by Eric Jan de Rooij: it was called Multi-Level Travel. Why not a "multi-level" experience?

The immediate tasks were to get the management board's buy-in and to prepare them for the retreat, the learning conference, and the larger ongoing effort of creating "Top Teams" to run the business. de Rooij (see spotlight) was tasked with finding a suitable location and weaving the outdoor components of the retreat into the heart, mind, and soul work.

Spotlight: Eric Jan de Rooij

Eric Jan de Rooij, whose résumé includes a degree in anthropology and a stint on the Dutch national hockey team, is the founder of Multi-Level Travel, the outfit that developed the flow of vistas and outdoor activities for VdBN team-building events in the Ardennes and later in Scotland and Jordan.

In his own words: "The thing we do, the thing I'm bringing in, is that we open people up. It's multi-level travel, not an outbreak. For me it works because you work at different levels, and you give space to people as they work on themselves, with others and as a whole group. The power of the program is much deeper and stronger when the leader says, 'I'm going to live it, I'm going to feel it and build it.'"

"My Story"

In early February, at a North Sea hotel, VdBN's managing board gathered with Mirvis and Ann Hoewing from FCE to talk about its own teamwork and preview elements that would be used at the team leader retreat. It included a role-play where board members argued for and against the prospects for company growth. There was a discussion of the characteristics of highly effective teams, and members completed a survey about their own team's effectiveness. The survey itself served as a wake-up call for the chairman and the board. Responses indicated that the members of the group were not being open and honest with one another, didn't function well as a team, and weren't providing leadership for the company.

The real awakening, however, had less to do with survey data and more to do with group dynamics. It was a fairly new board, having come together after the merger a year ago. Gunning opened the meeting by saying he'd never been on a board that actually worked together as a highly effective team, and that this was his goal, and he hoped FCE could help.

The board members then spent an hour reflecting on their upbringing and business life and writing "my story"—what had been the major effects in their lives? what did they stand for? what did they want to achieve? Their guidelines for telling their stories were to be authentic, to use "I" statements, and to reflect on their feelings—hopes and fears, highs and lows.

Later, as they sat in a circle, telling their stories in turn, they were asked to listen empathically, and to value differences. The first to really open up had been a director for eight years, a very respected person on the board who had played an important role in VdBN's transformation to date, Gunning recalled:

> As he talked, he was crying. This set the scene for me. Mine was the last story and I broke down too.
>
> An attendee was furious. She said, "There is a guy sitting there crying and you cannot even put your arms around him! You are a bunch of cold people." She was so shocked! I was shocked too, to realize how poor we were in the sense that we could not express our emotions or our empathy.

In the afternoon, the focus shifted to planning the team leader retreat. As David Saunders, a Covey consultant working alongside FCE, recalled:

> One of the directors commented that he'd expected to be really motivated, but was instead subdued and thoughtful. This seemed to be the mood of the group—they had shared an experience that went deep, and they were digesting it. Several said they'd learned things about each other that were entirely new.
>
> All this came from one brief, apparently simple exercise, "my story," that was somehow awakening a deeper level of emotional intelligence. A two-day board meeting on leadership the previous year had failed to achieve anything like this shift. Two weeks later, on a bus to the [team leader] event, the directors had an impromptu board meeting—without the chairman—and commented how easy and open and fruitful it had been.

The impact on the board was profound. This group—which had been so listless and had let their chairman dominate—suddenly started saying, "No, no, let's do this and let's do that." As one attendee described it, "The whole structure started to fall into place. In order to get to two thousand people, first we needed the management board on board. And then we needed to get the team leaders on board."

Rather than push teaming step-by-step down though the hierarchy, the board would create an organization-wide leadership team. This leadership team would be made up of leaders at all levels. Once formed, it included members from the marketing offices and the factory—whoever was responsible for supervising groups of people. Third shift foremen, people who had never even talked to board members or thought of themselves as company leaders, were invited to join the leadership team. As a board member put it, "You can talk with ten people, but you can't talk with fifteen hundred people regularly. It was magnificent to stimulate and motivate the complete workforce in the company."

The Ardennes

It was a crisp afternoon on February 25 when buses picked up the 180 VdBN team leaders at their different factory and business locations. They had been told that they would be away for three days, asked to bring warm clothes, and be prepared to rough it. The buses took them to the Ardennes forest in Belgium. As they alighted from the buses, they were each handed a rucksack with a winter jacket, given a lighted flare, and directed to go down a path through the dark woods. The path brought them to a clearing where the chairman stood with his torch and a team of FCE facilitators.

In the flickering torchlight, Gunning gave his opening speech on the need for Top Teams to run the business and achieve long-term growth:

> Our objective during the next few days is to develop into a team—
> a team of 180 leaders who run this company. One team—committed
> to the objective of growth.

We are going to talk with each other about how to achieve this; how we cooperate with each other, how we communicate, and how we handle conflicts. And we want to do that in an open and honest way.

Then in an exercise called "believers versus cynics," half the group brainstormed support of the vision of long-term growth and half brainstormed the contrary view. They joined up in pairs for an argument—each to defend their own side—to learn the concepts of debate, problem solving, conflict resolution, dialogue, and community as different ways to resolve conflict. The evening ended with a convivial feast by a roaring fire before adjourning to a nearby hotel.

The next morning the 180 leaders were taken to the ruins of a medieval monastery. After breakfast in the courtyard, they descended a long, difficult staircase into the catacombs. In that ancient setting they took a journey inward to reflect on their personal stories and explore their "emotional lifelines." As one of the consultants recalled the scene:

> Gunning started the process by showing the group the chart he had prepared of his emotional lifeline (which introduces this chapter). He talked through his life, starting the process by showing the group the chart. He began with the death of his father, then went into experiences in the military and his times in Unilever. The ups and downs in the life of a leader.

Emotional Lifelines

The idea behind the emotional lifeline is that organizational change begins with individuals.[2] As a precursor to team-building, the 180 present first needed to be able to get in touch with who they were themselves and to share that with one another. And in that space of speaking and listening to their own and each other's stories, a base of trust and respect could be built.

The discussion was unusual for a business gathering, and the intimate setting added to the impact. As Gunning recalled the experience:

> In the cellar of a ruin at Ardennes, I presented my emotional lifeline. It was not easy. I was in a little space in front of 180 team leaders, talking about the death of my father, an abusive stepfather, and the ups and downs of my adolescence. The silence became tangible. You touch people's hearts when you talk openly about your emotions.
>
> I will never forget a young woman in finance who was angry that I had not told my story sooner. There was an implicit message: "We would have forgiven you if we could have understood you."

The team leaders broke away, spreading out through the ruins to draw their own lifelines. Sitting on rock outcrops, relics of ancient walls, under trees, they worked first alone, then gathered in groups of two or three, and finally in their business and sourcing groups, to share with one another what they had done. They used this monastery space not so much to get close to God as to one another. At Antwerp Michelangelo's image of God reaching to Adam was a symbol of connection. In the Ardennes, this monastery would forever symbolize growing closer, together.

Many mentioned that they'd learned something about someone—or said something about themselves—that they hadn't heard or said in years of working together. Not all were comfortable with this level of intimacy. Sharing personal stories and releasing emotions requires people to be open, and gives peers information that leaves people vulnerable in the workplace. Some had the feeling that this level of sharing was dangerous.

"It creates a very focused moment of emotion," said a manufacturing director who was on the scene. "I really think that it had an impact because of the reactions I got afterwards. Many approached me." Others were not so sure. One sales service manager recalled thinking, "Is this a play? I am a pretty down-to-earth Dutchman.

Fine, I thought, one can tell stories like an emotional lifeline. OK, a lot of psychology, which was schemed in advance. What part is real, and what part is play? Who is the actor?"

"I think a lot of people grew there personally," said a marketing director who participated. "They realized who they are. Sharing your lifeline with people is a dramatic experience. First you have to think of your own life, which can be a dangerous experience. I think people grew—but translating that into business performance is difficult."

The rest of that first day in Ardennes built on the lifeline discussions with team-building initiatives drawn from Outward Bound–type programs—using ropes to transport objects, climbing over fences to retrieve material, building a rope bridge.[3] A rope zip into a canyon, a dusk-turned-night bike ride, and an evening of reflection in business and sourcing units completed the first day.

The Famous Fishbowl

One continuing challenge for VdBN was the teamwork of the management board. The script for the second day in the Ardennes called for the management board to debrief—in front of the other company leaders in what is called a "fishbowl" setting—how they worked as a team.[4]

As one of the consultants described it:

> The aim was to start a dialogue on how we're functioning in teams within each business. And the notion was that the board would take the leadership in that in the fishbowl. Suddenly they didn't want to do it. They had talked about it in the board meeting and looked at their ratings and said we're not a good group. We don't function well; we'll look foolish up here in front of team leaders.

In the end, the board decided to carry out the exercise and according to one of the consultants, "The experience was magnificent.

We could have found some other way to talk about the business. But it was the right time in the emotional staging and in the mythic story. It was time for the leaders to get up there and lead. And not just the chairman. They had a very powerful set of exchanges."

As Jaap Kalma, a marketing manager, told it:

> We sat in a big tent where a fishbowl took place. And we saw our leaders screw up, show vulnerability, and show understanding and learning. The chairman being scolded for mistreating his board members.
>
> It created a buzz, a feeling this was history being made. This was *real*, all this talk about authenticity. . . . The impact was that people dropped much of the professional masquerade, and in fact became more authentic.

The frankness of the discussion in the fishbowl had an immediate impact on the team leaders. For example, according to a sales manager who was present, when someone tried to make a point soon afterward, "He told the chairman, 'Listen, your team is the worst team in this company! That's where we should begin if we want teamwork.' I had a lot of respect for [him] because he dared to say that. People came out saying these guys are prepared to expose themselves."

The famous fishbowl was cited as a major breakthrough, forever changing the tone of company meetings. Moments of silence, the use of "I" statements, and candid dialogue became concepts that people sought to bring into their business conversations. One manager noted about the board, "It's a good thing that they were not afraid to show their vulnerability. We should do that as well." As Gunning saw it:

> That was the "miracle" that we needed. You can never create miracles. But you can create an environment that is inspirational, where it is safe to try things, where you can start to inquire. At the Ar-

dennes, we created that space through the lifelines and a manage-ment team exposing themselves in a fishbowl in front of their peo-ple. Vulnerability is so powerful. You saw all the units become connected, there was a different tone of voice.

"It was fascinating to watch," said one of the consultants. "The barriers were all down, if only for a brief while. It reminds me of the story in the Bible of the temple veil being torn in two—which sep-arated the 'Holy of Holies' from the regular folks. There could no longer be any secret about them and what they were up to. Some-thing very definitely shifted, even though it's hard to put a finger on it."

From Teams to Tribes

That night, following another evening bike ride, the community building became very real as managers constructed their campsite at the top of a hill in a windy, cold drizzle. A large A-frame and smaller tents for sleeping are fashioned out of poles, planks, and tarp, forming a circular village with a huge fire in the middle.

Once the structures are built and sleeping places secured, people stand around the fire, feasting, drinking, singing, beating on drums, being entertained by a troupe of jugglers and stilt-walkers, and sa-voring the company of new friends. They are cold, tired—many had not slept the night before. They huddle together. Rank is on hold. There is an enormous amount of reflection as acknowledgment of what needs to be done as people talk quietly in pairs or small groups. "The scene is bizarre, primal," said one of the consultants.

We are in a windswept encampment on a hilltop in the middle of win-ter. Our group has built its shelter for the night. Fires are lit to keep the dark at bay, and wild animals. A fire ritual is played out. There are drums for everyone. We try different rhythms. We make noise. This is not about twentieth-century industry. We are a tribe. . . .

A man comes up to me and starts to tell me that he has just been talking with a marketing director. His team at the factory has pulled out the stops for a project on a new product, and he told the director it would be nice if they could be acknowledged. Not a material reward, just recognition. The director suggested he come to the factory and thank them. There are almost tears in this man's face. This man is a manager who has worked years for Van den Bergh. And he says this is the first time he has ever talked to a director.

Chapter 7

Community or Cult?

> Things changed drastically when Tex said, "We
> need growth, and we need *everybody* to grow the
> business." Growth was something he brought to us:
> a really different way of thinking and working.
>
> —*Team leader*

The whole company is shut down for the day for the 1998 Learning Conference on March 6. All eighteen hundred VdBN employees are bussed to Brabanthallen, a convention center in den Bosch, near one of the factories. Everyone is wearing identical sweats emblazoned with the Learning Conference logo: "Competing for Our Future." A huge exhibition hall has been divided up for the event. In one corner there is an auditorium-like area, complete with tiered seating, theater lighting, and three huge backlit projection screens. As the employees enter the scene, a Dutch singer is doing a Tina Turner impression to warm up the crowd—"You're Simply the Best" blares over the sound system. It's 9 A.M. and the atmosphere is electric.

Then as the action unfolds, the crowd witnesses something quite unprecedented: The chairman is not in the spotlight.

Sharing the Spotlight

In the first year of VdBN's transformation, and certainly at company gatherings, the other managing directors have been definitely eclipsed by their chairman. Now they are the headliners at the 1998 Learning Conference with an idea they proposed themselves: Two board members are going to present their lifelines; two others will talk about their "masks" (drawings of themselves that symbolize what lies behind the masks they wear at work). The intent is to demonstrate that they are serious about openness—modeling what the teams will be doing shortly and taking big emotional risks themselves. "It's all in Dutch, but you don't need to understand the words," recalls David Saunders, one of the consultants attending the event, "you can feel the emotion."

"One director has them on the edge of their seats—You could literally have heard a pin drop," Saunders recounted. "He was telling everyone about being born during World War II and how he never saw his father until after the war because his father had been arrested as a suspected Nazi collaborator. From that day on the director's life changed forever. It was an awful disgrace, the family had to move schools and keep the curtains in their house drawn. His father was later acquitted, but the damage was done. He also told a story about a point in his career when he was working with a person who cheated and stabbed him in the back. He combined these two events to explain how trust was broken in him for life."

"It was only then that I realized why this guy was so independent in his work," recalled Gunning. "He rejected interdependency purely because of his horrible experiences. This guy broke down on stage in front of eighteen hundred people. The effect was so profound. He had been a leader for eight years. People thought they knew him. When they realized they did not know him, they felt ashamed. He had gotten his Ph.D. for his father. These things really hit the audience."

Another director came on stage. He was raised in Belgium and had gone to boarding school. He told the audience that in Belgium boarding schools are not just for rich kids, but also young criminal kids. He told them that these young criminals beat him up every day. He had resolved that he never was going to be beaten up again.

Next up were two directors who demonstrated the masks they wore to create their personae at work. One was the finance director, who was not the most open character, who described and demonstrated his attachment to his family. The other was an Englishman who never showed any emotion. "Even in the exercise he did not really show himself," said one observer, "but he became very emotional about his relationship with his wife. He showed everyone her picture. At last we saw a human part of him."

Then eighteen hundred people began to work on their own emotional lifelines. "I will never forget it," said an event organizer.

> Normally there is an enormous noise in these halls with that many people working. But, you heard nothing at all! People were drawing, concentrating. I could not believe the intensity with which they approached this task.

Telling Their Stories

As engaged as many were in telling their life stories, the discomfort in others was noticeable. For some, it seemed to be a matter of culture. "For Americans it might be much easier," said a union leader. "The Dutch find it really difficult when it comes to such things. They don't talk about income or personal stuff easily. Other cultures might be more open. Especially the old Dutch people can't cope with it."[1]

Also tricky for some was that the boss was asking them to do it. "You can't really refuse," said one. "It is hard to know where to draw the line." And some just wanted to keep their distance. "I do not want people to know me that well," said a Unox operator. "I want to have my private life. I do not want to wear a mask but I do not want you to know everything about me. If you care about me as a person, you must also respect my privacy."

Several said they could deal with the emotional discussion themselves but questioned it for others. "For me," said a Uniquisine employee, "it was OK but I know a lot of people had problems with it. The emotional things, too deep into personal things. And of course they said you could go only as far as you like, but not all the people know where to stop."

In large part, though, employees understood—and accepted—the premise that if you know one another better emotionally, you can work better together as a team. "I wanted to share those personal feelings and experiences," said a marketing manager, "because we were already on a strong platform. I thought that it helped to build even stronger personal relations." To persuade others of the benefits of opening up, many pointed to the example of a person who had difficulties with his team members because he had to take off to go to the hospital very often, but he hadn't told his colleagues why. "When he shared in the lifeline session that his wife was in the hospital dying from cancer," said Alex Korbee, the company physician, "they all helped him."

Being Yourself

The rest of the day was devoted to team-building exercises, familiar to all from prior gatherings, plus a new community-building practice, circles of reflection. In these small group discussions, team leaders were advised that they could not lead their groups into community. But they, and anyone else, could express their thoughts, call for silence, or reflect on what was happening in the group. The intent was to create a safe environment for reflection. Said one of the team leaders: "Only in a safe environment, where leadership at every level is sincere and professional, can people really be themselves, challenge issues, and take initiative. This brings out the best in people." The day ended with the trademark festive party of the company's Learning Conferences—with lots of food, song, and dance.

The highlights of the event, though controversial, were sharing personal stories in work teams and practicing community-building principles.[2] The learning conference was a memorable experience that redefined the company's leadership, strengthened the interactions between people, and deepened their thinking and feelings toward one another in the workplace. "After this learning conference the company was changed," said the chairman:

There was openness. People saw that the management team was also human. I had told them that I could not grow this business. I could help, bring strategy, and be a coach, but they could not expect me to grow this business. I told them, "You can do it, just be yourself." And that is what we did.

Cascading Teaming

After the Ardennes and the Learning Conference, people were more and more aware that they had to do it as a team—"Everybody together, the weakest held by the strongest," in the words of a Nassaukade factory team leader. Team building continued to cascade into the organization. Business units adopted team structures and team leaders in factories trained with their groups.

The 180 team leaders met several times during 1998 to continue their development as a leadership group. In the spring, for instance, they completed a self-assessment on the level of development of their work teams. They also learned to coach one another on their progress as team leaders. And already they were reaping some of the rewards of teaming. Said one, "As a team leader you start to think about the company, initiate things, and function better. You get more satisfaction out of your work. It becomes more fun when you are allowed as a group to take decisions about your work and budgets."

In the fall, the team leaders spent a day outdoors biking on country roads and picking apples in an orchard. Updates of different team-building activities were given. They heard about other teams that had gone on outbreaks, and they learned from one of the team leaders about how team building had spread in the Nassaukade factory:

I went with each of my three groups to the Ardennes' forests where we did exercises and lived together for three days. The exercises were designed in such a way that you needed each other. If one was not helping the other, the whole team could not go on. You had to help each other and that was eye-opening.

We went a long way with teamwork. Now they are all talking to each other and saying: "If something is not going right, we must talk it through." In the past, this was impossible. You would never tell a colleague that unless he changes his behavior he has to get out of the team.

To build the infrastructure to support team building, Hans van't Sant recruited team coaches, had them trained by FCE, and formed a training unit. Geert Maassen, an old and respected hand in the Nassaukade factory, joined with Ankie van Lindt and another trainer to serve as coaches to the team leaders. van't Sant and Hans Cornuit also offered Covey courses to teams. Community-building and learning organization principles were incorporated into the Covey training sessions. There was considerable talk of popular management books and buzzwords among team leaders as they all raced to keep pace with their peers and develop their people.

Cult of Change?

Spouting new language and promoting team building as a way of life, the 180 team leaders became more and more visible and vocal throughout VdBN. On the plus side, many saw the more communal board and newly dubbed team leaders as the standard-bearers of the company's current challenge of "Competing for our Future." On the other side, some were feeling that a cult of change was taking over the company.[3]

"This whole thing made me think of the Bhagwan," said a Nassaukade team leader. "How can we ask people to go look so deep down into their soul? I don't think that it is a good thing." "Mass manipulation!" said a marketing manager. "That is how I react to these kinds of things. In the beginning it felt as a conformity thing." "It felt suddenly like a cult," echoed a factory manager, adding:

There was the "preacher" standing on a podium telling us how we should be. In the beginning, it felt like a uniform thing. But, in the end, of course, it was actually about being yourself.

In time, even some of the most vocal skeptics began to appreciate that self-disclosure and team building were effective ways to get a group mobilized. Said one:

> In the beginning we all approached it with great caution. I feared that they wanted to talk me into something.
>
> After the Ardennes, maybe in just a couple of weeks, I saw that there was openness and trust. I started believing that together we could grow this business. If we hadn't gone through the Ardennes and shared our stories, it would have been so much more difficult to achieve this kind of trust. Who knows, maybe even impossible.

One thing was clear: In the name of teamwork, the chairman and the management board, by their example, were asking people to reveal elements of themselves—their history and emotions—that many had always kept personal and private. Strategic reviews, business talk, and even some of the events in VdBN to this point had been aimed at changing mindsets. The Ardennes and the 1998 Learning Conference—and community building in their aftermath throughout VdBN—addressed "heartsets." A key element of all was to demand that the leaders show their emotions and share their life stories.

"Leaders have to manage emotions to be effective," said Cornuit. "They need emotional depth and literacy. Leaders should learn to speak about their own emotions. And lifelines can help them to understand themselves."

Emphasis on Business *and* People

Throughout 1998 improvement efforts continued at all organizational levels and strong business results were being recorded in the marketing and sourcing units. In particular, the Foods business unit was showing excellent volume and profit growth. Work continued at a steady pace to develop "highly effective people" through Covey training and "highly effective teams." In their drive to build their own teams and grow, most team leaders focused on their own people and challenges. The cost was the lack of a collective leadership agenda. There were disconnects between the sourcing and business units on goals, priorities, and responsibilities. And there were miscommunications across business units and between factories.

The second half of 1998 was the time to think about what would be the next stage for VdBN. "That hadn't been done properly," observed a quality manager. "The target setting was too much on individual units or individual parts of the business. This did not really fit enough with a shared goal at the total company level. The only thing that held us together in the end were the trading results." As a sales services manager put it:

> Only at the management board level do they operate together. In the business units people never look to other units for advice: "How do you tackle this type of problem? How do you act on this or that?" You may see teamwork in sales, or in category management, within each business unit team. . . . But I don't think the account manager of Fats talks with the account manager of Foods.

These questions of connection and communication were the backdrop for the management conference ending 1998, again held in Antwerp. There a subset of the 180 team leaders, those running business and sourcing units, met to talk shop, define roles and goals for the next year, and continue building community. The chairman outlined some of the of the key principles or groundrules for the meeting:

- It is very easy to start talking about "us," about the group. So it is important that we use "I" statements in a sense that you truly speak out what you have to say.
- You don't have to speak to listen actively. It is a matter of being present.
- If you think the energy level is too low then you just ask for a process stop. You say, "Look, my energy is flowing out; can we talk about what's happening or get a five-minute stop?"

- If you run a business there will be moments that you will disagree with a colleague. You will disagree with the boss and
  then there will come a moment that somebody says let's agree
  to disagree. You have got to realize, it doesn't mean you've
  lost. It doesn't mean there is a loss of face or that you've been
  overruled. No, it means that a decision had to be taken.

"It's important for people to know that in the end decisions
have to be taken in order for the business to move onwards," he
added. "You will continuously have differences of opinion. Get
them on the table and debate them deeply."

This meeting incorporated another new practice: Each unit presented the business plan of their sister unit. The Foods business
unit, for instance, presented the Food factories' plans and vice versa.
The same pairing was done for the Fats sourcing and selling units.
This approach was designed to make interdependent units familiar
with one another's objectives and provide the opportunity for feedback and change.

The communication process included fishbowls for debriefing
the plans and the development agendas for their sister units. The
benefits of mixing business and team talk, hard and soft analyses,
and head and heart orientations were notable to those that attended. As one marketing director described it:

> The most important thing is that people are thinking in total busi-
> ness terms again. Everybody can relate his personal work, his task,
> his project, or whatever to a business gain or to progress. So the mar-
> keting person is not just thinking about television commercials, the
> development person is not just thinking about products. Instead
> everybody is talking about building the business.

The challenge now was not just to grow as separate units, categories, and individuals. The aim was to grow and learn collectively—
by sharing ideas, teaching each other, and transforming all of the
business together. The new emphasis was on *connectedness*.

Chapter 8

The McVan den Bergh Clan

You can work on transformation one by one, team
by team. But that is not fast enough.

　　　　　　　　　　　　　　　　　—*Tex Gunning*

It is February 1999 on the historic Culloden battlefield, where the
Scottish clans joined forces to fight the English in 1746. Wearing a
kilt and carrying a shield, Gunning greets the 180 VdBN team leaders. He begins their three-day "leadership journey" by reminding
them what they had set out to do:

> About one and a half years ago we decided in the management
> board that it was impossible for us alone to run this business. That's
> why we identified 180 leaders to lead this business. And you are the
> ones to lead eighteen hundred people to achieve growth year after
> year.

In the background are the distinct and moving sounds of the
Scottish bagpipe. Two flags flutter in the fierce wind: one with the
VdBN symbol and another with a new slogan—*Legacy of Growth*.
Hours ago in Holland these team leaders had boarded two charter
planes for a destination unknown to them. When they touched
down at the Inverness airport in northern Scotland, they were
bursting with excitement and enthusiasm—especially those who
had never before been on an airplane or off the European mainland.

Gathering the McTeams

Scotland was an apt choice for this gathering of team leaders who needed to band together and find their own clan spirit. For the Dutch, Scotland holds a mystic appeal. It is beautiful but remote, with jagged mountains and deep lochs worn by the rough North Atlantic climate, and replete with legends and lore—kings, castles, songs, and peoples known by their clan names and tartans. Vestiges of the ancient past continue today: Scotland's highland games feature physical competition along with folk art and entertainment in a festival atmosphere.

The themes of clans, games, legend, and lore shaped the design of the 1999 team leader gathering. The event stressed the need for VdBN's unit leaders to bring together teams that were independently successful. To bring the theme to life, team leaders assembled at this historic place and steeped themselves in the clan mystique as they walked the battlefield, learned its significance, tried their hand at swordplay, and breathed in the cold, damp air.

Being together as a whole was the goal in Scotland, so to begin each business unit was designated a clan. Each clan—the McSoups, McMeats, McSauces, and McSpreads—created its own flag and developed a yell to identify itself. Then they were given their challenge—to join forces as the McVan den Bergh community.

The script to bring the still-too-separate business and sourcing units together in clanlike relationships to carry on the "legacy of growth" had seemed appropriate and attainable on paper. But unpredictable elements, in nature and in man, conspired to constrain accomplishment of these objectives.

Inauspicious Beginnings

On the first night, in a massive tent near a castle by Loch Ness, the scenario called for the chairman to speak to his own legacy of growth. Following his example, everyone would then write out their own legacies and share them with one another. But Gunning was dispirited about personal problems, and it showed in his presentation.

As one manager recalled, "We had a funny start when Tex was not connected well when he was talking." Other conditions distracted people too—the sound system kept cutting in and out, and a very loud wind howled. The subsequent writing and sharing of stories was ragged. A year earlier, the lifeline exercise had sparked great energy and built connections. This exercise, by comparison, went flat. Afterward the individual groups retreated quickly to their own tents to escape the bitter wind and rain.

That night, hurricane-force winds collapsed most of the tents and shredded the large one used as the common meeting place. Everyone woke early, moved to a barn, and held a community meeting where they voiced their discomfort and frustration. After a while, the process of sharing their views of the experience so far helped them to rally around the overall agenda. Spirits were high as they broke into smaller groups to embark on team outings—hiking, biking, canoeing—with the idea of coming together that evening in mixed groups at campsites to share comradeship and talk of new business opportunities.

Unfortunately, that day's weather was miserable too, even by Scottish standards. At least half the groups could not do what they planned because it was either too windy or too wet, and then their tents blew over again. Every group improvised: some staying in farmhouses, some going to hotels, and others camping out alone.

Instead of coming together as one large clan, the groups grew even more disconnected from one another. Some had a grand time while others were miserable; some got together for work, others for play, and still others not at all. The individual group experience had been uneven, to say the least, and an overall community connection seemed beyond reach. The only shared experience was that they had all survived the weather.

"In Scotland some people talked about themselves but others didn't," observed a Calvé team leader. "Every unit moved out on its own. We did not have enough time to pull them together and set expectations. The space we were in was too big. There was too much walking around, not enough talking."

"It was raining very hard and we had to sleep in tents," recalled a safety manager from Nassaukade.

> In our group we decided we were not going to sleep in the tent anymore, because it was cold, wet, and windy. We saw a gas station with a canteen and we went there. There were about twenty-five people from marketing there. One guy arranged for us all to sleep there. Then somebody else thought we should play some music. In about thirty minutes all the tables were pushed aside, the lights dimmed and we were partying. And this was not planned in the program but everybody is still talking about it. We had fun together, just plain fun. When we had a fishbowl on the last day, John said, "I've been working at Unilever for eleven years now and I've never had so much fun with my colleagues as last night."

The View from the Top

The third day, at last, was glorious. Exhausted from lack of sleep or worn down by partying, the various clans met at the foot of the Corrain, a famous mountain on the Isle of Skye. En masse, the team leaders embarked on a two-hour climb up a steep trail through the muddy and stony highlands terrain. Up and down, through gullies and up the sharp hills, many struggled to finish the demanding hike.

At the summit, there was a sense of collective accomplishment when all finally arrived. The sun broke through the high clouds, and in time with a bagpiper, the reunited clans shouted out their yells and waved their flags. Everyone had made it to the top, and they had done it as one large team—the McVan den Bergh clan!

One image that would stay with everyone was the big circle they then formed at the top of Corrain. They took each other's hands and counted off: one, two, one, two. . . . The ones leaned into the circle, the twos leaned backward, and the only thing that kept them all from falling down was the support they got from everyone holding on to everyone else in the circle. The message was powerful: "We have to do it together."

Walking down the mountain brought other powerful images, as many of those who had struggled up the mountain now struggled with the descent: One of the oldest factory hands, Bram van Twilt— a traditional Dutchman, the antithesis of many there—being helped to the bottom by some of the youngest team leaders; Fats category manager Conny Braams—a counterpoint to the angry young men— fighting exhaustion as she slowly works her way down the slope. When the last finally made it down, cheers and more cheers—from VdBN and UVGN people, from McSoups and McMeats, and from old and young.

The team leaders were now, as one recalled it, "Everybody together, the weakest held by the strongest." That evening was the beginning of a new kind of conversation in VdBN.[1] Different views on how men and women were effective, matters of age and gender, issues of work and personal life, all were raised and talked about— and became part of VdBN's leadership development agenda. Sharing ideas about helping and supporting one another, they talked deeply about the difficulty of transformation. Many had signed on at Unilever under the ethic of working eight-hour days, doing your job, and then getting home to family, friends, a personal life. All this had changed and now challenged their connections to their spouses and children. Life was on the business agenda, and vice versa.[2]

Behind the Scenes

As the team leaders rode together on the train back to Inverness airport they began to think about the upcoming Learning Conference. The nature of what they learned in going to Scotland would be hard to communicate. It was made harder by the skepticism that many of the workers back at factories and offices felt about the trip. Why had their supervisors traveled so far from home, and what was the benefit for the business? How would they communicate that the spending was worth it and bring a benefit to those that didn't go?

"If you are part of the team leaders of course it's tremendously nice to go to Scotland," said a sales services manager. "But after you come back to the work floor you have to explain to your colleagues what you are going to do. You feel skepticism from those who did not share your experience. I don't know how to handle that." And how to meld the sense of community they had experienced in Scotland with the advances in team autonomy in many parts of the company?

Change in the Factories

The team leader events and the company-wide Learning Conferences and Covey training had provided the overall momentum for change in the company. Team building and TPM (Total Preventive Maintenance, or Teams Perform More) were the everyday mechanisms driving transformation, particularly in the factories. "The real big change in the factories started with giving people responsibility for the future of the factories," said Synhaeve.

> They had to take responsibility for the performance of their factory and start competing with colleagues in Europe and with other competitors. What gave them the confidence to take responsibility and empowered them to take responsibility was TPM.

It had not been an easy road. "In the beginning some people found it difficult that they couldn't just throw it back over the fence to middle management," said a safety manager. "Also when you make people redundant, the people who stay over have to work harder. So we had to go over a hill. We tackled that 60 percent by TPM and 40 percent by team building."

"When TPM started, people thought, 'Here comes another project,'" said another safety manager. "But gradually a whole new way of thinking developed. And quite quickly we saw some results.

There was real commitment of management. That made people think: 'Hey, this is great, this must be it, this one must be real.'"

What boosted the impact of TPM in sourcing units was the continuous investment in team building. The success of the "highly effective teams" initiative led to the evolution of the team concept. And by the time the team leaders went to Scotland in 1999, several teams had evolved into self-managing groups. Their success, in turn, was dependent on continued investment in individual training—the idea being, as van Lindt, a team trainer, put it, "Personal growth leads to business growth and business growth leads to personal growth. So if you start with the individual, you have more impact on the teams and as a team you have more impact on the organization."

"TPM and team building are two things you can't separate from each other," observed a safety manager, "they reinforce each other."

> And you get even more motivated when you go further. You have the lower costs, higher efficiencies so people are more enthusiastic and take even more responsibility into their own hands. A few years ago we moved to autonomous groups and told shift-leaders to deal with it. It's even clearer that teams have to find their own solutions because there's nobody to help them. We are in the middle of teaching autonomous groups to learn to look at the whole picture.

Connecting the Teams

In the beginning the team leaders were all busy with team building within their own departments. Then they started experimenting with cross-functional teams. "So you work on a project where one is responsible for quality and another for the technical aspects," said a department manager by way of example. "This was unimaginable a couple of years ago."

All sorts of new tasks and responsibilities were pushed down to the workers. "They could no longer leave their heads at the entrance to the factory," said one of the team leaders. "So renewed energy was flowing everywhere. The culture changed too." "We now go out at least twice a year to do something fun," reported one of the plant operators. "This never happened in the past. So you realize that you want to spend time together outside work and that the department has actually become a team."

Slowly, a sense of community developed: You are not alone because you can rely on your team, and you are also part of something bigger than a team. Working in teams redefined relationships at work, creating a feel for the larger whole. As a VdBN internal consultant observed:

> The community feeling developed: I am not just part of Unox, I am part of VdBN. Now there is sharing of resources and knowledge. In 1997 this was impossible. There was very little teamwork between the sites. People didn't even want to see each other. It's completely different now.

From Top Down to Bottom Up

Over time, the complexity of creating a relevant all-company annual Learning Conference had increased. But with the increasing emotional and intellectual sensitivity, the conferences were linked closer to the mood of the organization and to what needed to be accomplished.

As the team leaders exchanged ideas for the 1999 Learning Conference on their way back from Scotland, there was a growing realization that they would have to play a larger part than ever before in preparing for the event and running the show. As one of the QA managers recalled:

> All the events—the Learning Conferences, the team leaders' events, etc. . . . helped very much the creation of VdBN as one company. It also helped develop the teams and leadership practices that nowadays we take for granted.
>
> But I felt that this was done with the chairman determining what is good for the rest of the business. That may be necessary in

the beginning, but as soon as your people start to develop, you have to accept that they have to play a role in designing these events, and make sure that the design fits what is happening in the different units.

This time, the team leaders agreed, they would own more of the agenda for the Learning Conference and be responsible for designing and doing experiential learning activities with their own teams.

Learning Conference 1999

The February 1999 Learning Conference began with the teams from the business and sourcing units gathering at various spots in eastern Holland—with their bicycles. At the appointed time they mounted their bikes and pedaled to Gelredome, an indoor superstadium in nearby Arnhem, to meet with their colleagues. Imagine the scene: Eighteen hundred bicycles entering en masse to encounter the bright lights, lively music, stage full of local entertainers, and all the food and festivity surrounding them.

As was now customary, the day started and ended as a big party. In between were working and learning sessions. Also expected was the chairman's review of the company's prior-year results and its goals for 1999. In closing, he reminded everyone of their role in the company's agenda for the future and growth:

> We need each other to build a business that can continually grow. It is through growth that we can grow as individuals. For that to happen you have to ask yourselves how can I as an individual, or how can we as a team, contribute to growth?

Then something completely different: The team leaders took over and led their groups through the exercises, discussions, and activities they had designed themselves. Finally, to emphasize their connectedness, the teams took turns in karaoke—singing each other's songs as the words were projected onto the big screen.

As the last activity of the day before the closing party, the entire company saw the concept of "we have to do it together" brought to life. On the vast floor of the stadium, each unit set up video boxes of specific colors in the designated spots—creating the "world's largest domino effect." Started by pushing just one box, they all fell, one by one, row by row, to form the logos of each unit. And encompassing these, in turn, were the fallen "dominos" forming the logo of Van den Bergh Nederland. The result was projected onto the big screen where everyone could follow the progress and see how it all fit together.

The ideas of getting the "whole system" together to hear a common message, work on current problems, build new capabilities, and prepare for the future were drawn from the body of best practices in change management that had gained currency over the past decade. So had the value of first developing an understanding of and commitment to change in a leadership body and then cascading that message though an organization. But there was—and still is—not much in the way of tested practice on how to design and stage large-group processes that simultaneously inform and stimulate as well as develop individual and collective capabilities, let alone create a deep sense of community.

The magic of events in VdBN—and the "miracles," as some referred to them, that were experienced—came from continuous experimentation and learning, a mix of planning and improvisation, and making space for serendipity. This was not the application of management science, per se, or based on a cookbook. Rather, event organizers also referenced principles of design, folklore, the performing arts, and various spiritual traditions. The chairman had his own take on things:

> I always see three major things in these events. One is that you bring the people in a certain space so that you can approach them emotionally. And then you start to integrate intellect and emotion. You cannot do this in the office.

The second thing is that you benefit from the dynamics of large groups to accelerate the process. Plus you have to manage the skepticism. By bringing the cynics and skeptics into these events, you see that they begin to move with the large group. Everyone becomes connected to the transformation process.

And the third is that it is a gift. If you do it properly, people accept this as a gift. It is a reward of sorts—the travel itself, the experience, and the investment into personal growth.

These ideas had guided the evolution of the team leader events and the all-company Learning Conferences from the beginning. But they were put into action at VdBN in a new way when team leaders joined together after Scotland to help design and run a learning conference that engaged the entire organization. Bringing the leadership together en masse provided a common orientation and mobilized them to lead change. And bringing all eighteen hundred employees together to hear the message of connectedness straight from the team leaders provided the scale and scope necessary to speed things up. In the words of a Calvé operator:

> To a lot of people the chairman still comes across as the man from the ivory tower. But with eighteen hundred people in the hall, when your own team leader, an ordinary guy from the factory, gets up and says: "Guys, we have to take a good look at ourselves and make improvements, otherwise we will not survive next year. We have to change and set ourselves some goals." That makes an impact.

Part IV

Transforming
the Business

Chapter 9

Growing a Market

Foods

> Building a kitchen office was a great idea. If you are
> a food company, make sure it's visible that you have
> a passion for food.
>
> —*Hans Cornuit, HR director*

There was an aura of mystery about the hammering, sawing, and clutter of construction behind the plastic curtain sealing off the chairman's corner office at VdBN. Months before, all nearby offices at VdBN HQ had been demolished and replaced by an airy space. Soon carts of new furniture were wheeled in to this space, along with flip charts, computers with Internet connections, a monitor for reporting up-to-the-minute stock prices and other business news, and who knew what else. Meanwhile Tex was holed up in his secretary's office or else buzzing away in the roomy new workroom cum café. What was going on in his office space?

It still wasn't altogether clear when the curtain first rose on the renovation and the management board assembled for their regular meeting. Near the windows overlooking the river they saw a sleek desk, ergonomic office chair, and a small sitting area with a couch, two chairs, and some art deco–type end tables—all ultramodern, the Dutch version of Scandinavian.

In stark contrast, at the center of the room, the board saw a long wooden table. It would work fine for meetings, but it looked like—and indeed was—an old-fashioned farmhouse kitchen table. The inside wall was taken up by a refrigerator, microwave, oven, and stove sectioned off by a peninsula containing a sink and dishwasher, cabinets stocked with glasses, plates, and silverware, and, upon inspection, stockpiles of packaged food—snacks, soups, entrees, sauce mixes, beverages, and more. Someone pointed to pots and pans, and the board members soon found themselves opening jars and cans, and chopping, stirring, baking, and grilling their luncheon meal.

The board dined that noon at the old kitchen table, talking about their food and its preparation—and a bit about their own teamwork—along with their regular business agenda. At future meetings, one board member would be assigned responsibility to shop for lunch and orchestrate its cooking. Working with a limited budget, equal to what the average Dutch household might spend, the designated chef had to purchase a variety of food products—Unilever's as well as those of its competitors. The board's fellowship deepened as they cooked and ate together regularly. So did their firsthand knowledge of the "consumer experience" and the quality, taste, and ease of preparing what the marketplace had to offer.

A Passion for Food

With the revolution in the Foods unit complete and the troika firmly in charge, the next step was to revisit the Strategic Programme 2002 begun in UVGN and reconsider it in light of VdBN's brands. John Zealy, one of the team's external advisers, summed up what was happening with food trends in Holland:

> The food we eat is no longer a definition of ourselves. Twenty years ago, you had full-time housewives who went shopping, spent virtually the whole day cooking, and served a meal to which everyone in the family turned up. And you all ate Sunday lunch together. At that time, food was a defining characteristic of a family and a nation.
>
> Today, the typical person spends fifteen minutes preparing dinner for which he or she will be lucky if more than two people eat together at the same time. Food and the way we consume food no longer defines national identity.

Next the team looked at its current product portfolio. They found a fragmented mix of brands and marketing concepts, with growth opportunities that varied significantly from product to product and market to market. "Some categories can grow 5 percent versus let's say 60 percent for others," observed a sales manager. "We have young brands that we have to grow rapidly and we have mature brands that demand attention and support. And we operate in multiple channels: supermarkets, retail stores, and out-of-home." The team also recognized that aiming for growth across all brands would lead to internal competition for resources and deprive some groups of the depth and investment needed to exploit higher-growth opportunities.

With a fresh perspective on their product portfolio and distribution channels, the team found opportunities in the growing tendency of people to consume food outside their home, to snack and graze throughout the day, and, in Holland at least, to favor "international" foods. "So instead of worrying 'How can I maintain my market share?' we said, 'Let's focus on growth and use our brains and imagination to realize that,'" one marketeer recalled.

To begin to get the necessary depth and apply their brains and imagination, the Foods team launched a series of consumer studies. Inquiries into the emotional appeal of foods, analyses of demographic and consumption trends, and many face-to-face encounters with consumers in focus groups led to what one termed a "paradigm shift" in the Foods group.

Looking Outside In

The team began to look at business opportunities from the outside in and think about their products in terms of flesh-and-blood consumers rather than as, say, product categories targeted at particular market segments. "All of a sudden we could build the brand concept from the consumer and what's happening in the market," recalled Bauke Rouwers (see spotlight), marketing director in Foods. "Then it all went really quickly."

Spotlight: Bauke Rouwers

Bauke Rouwers was a high-potential Unilever manager destined for a global career path to senior management. As a marketing manager in VdBN, he joined the troika heading Foods uncertain about Tex's style but every bit as committed to growing the business. He had a strong people-feeling and bold aspirations to "create an environment where people can make a difference" and "develop that almost magical spirit by which we can achieve the unthinkable."

Rouwers led the Foods group through its portfolio analyses and emphasized the need for the team to look outside in. "Normally we would focus on the nitty-gritty and then look outward and at our star opportunities. Here we did it the other way around. This clarified our vision and sharpened our strategy." Somewhat shy and low-key, in contrast to other leaders in Foods, Rouwers was credited by several young marketeers with giving them the trust and the space needed to bring their ideas to market.

"Looking outside instead of inside" also freed up creativity and energy in the Foods group. Said Rowers:

> Somebody made a good comparison. It's like a big bucket of crabs where as soon as one crab wants to get out another one, also trying to get out, pulls it back down. Everybody is so busy with themselves and looking inside that nobody breaks out. But if you really come from the outside in, and develop a vision like making Cup-a-Soup into a daily habit, all of a sudden you get people benchmarking themselves against the outside world.

This new way of thinking began to spread through the Foods group. "More and more," said a young brand manager, "they began to ask themselves, 'OK, what do we have to do for this specific consumer?'" The team translated their answers to this question into an energizing vision for competing for the future. Building on the *Star Trek* theme, the Foods unit pledged to "boldly go where no one has gone before":

- To develop people, brands and capabilities to compete for growth year after year
- To develop new markets and take market and distribution channel share away from competitors

"We began visioning what it was going to look like," reported one of the marketeers. "We used it as a guide for deciding what to do and what not to do, to make choices and keep focused on where we wanted to be."

Focusing on Stars

Boston Consulting Group's strategy matrix, which compares growth and profit opportunities, helped to organize Foods managers' thinking about growth opportunities (Exhibit 9.1).[1] They categorized their products using this matrix, and then developed appropriate strategic plans. Bauke recalled:

> We translated it into the BCG matrix, which is nothing special, but it worked. And then we assembled this portfolio strategy and we got together for half a day with this on the table. We finalized it and everybody agreed on it.
>
> We realized that going for new products in the new markets would bring only 1 percent chance of success, and improving on current products in current markets would almost bring 100 percent of success. So we decided not to build any extra categories and to focus on the categories we already have. We would try to innovate in those categories and make them grow. ·

Exhibit 9.1 Boston Consulting Group Matrix

	Low Profit	High Profit
High Growth	Prospects	Stars
Low Growth	Dogs	Cash Cows

Foods had two stars in its portfolio: Liptonice and Cup-a-Soup.[2] They got all the attention, all the people, and all the money that they needed. "Once that was taken care of we started working on other things," said Bauke. To make the priorities clear, they set specific growth targets for each category. The stars, the team decided, would need to grow at least 20 percent per annum. "Meanwhile people who had to manage products like the smoked meats," explained a marketer, "would get a target of 5 percent growth—which is an equally big stretch goal. So that way everybody felt challenged and motivated."

A number of products, including Unox pork sausages, were identified as "cash cows"—to be milked as profit generators. Some of the "dogs" (products with low growth potential, and with limited profitability) were delisted. The fourth category—"prospects"—had growth potential but low current profitability. The Foods business would make headway in this sector with its chef-and-restaurant business (see Chapter Eleven).

Growing Share: Liptonice

Seeing their greatest growth opportunities in the out-of-home market, Foods managers decided to offer their underexploited branded products to consumers-on-the-go. One of the first brands to be considered was Liptonice—the ice tea beverage offered in the United States and United Kingdom—which had not taken off in the Netherlands.

To get it going, recalled an account manager, the team started by looking outside in for benchmarking in this category:

> For the beverage business you don't have to invent too much. It's a very transparent market with five big players in the market. The biggest brand in the beer business is Heineken, which makes the rules. And for soft drinks Coca-Cola makes the rules. You analyze and investigate these markets and you learn. You don't have to reinvent that business. So we used the distribution tactics of Heineken and the brand policy of Coca-Cola.

A product group was formed to take charge of Liptonice, given autonomy and profit-and-loss accountability, and told to run with it. Liptonice was relaunched as "healthy refreshment" and positioned as an alternative to cola drinks.

"The team had the insight to see Liptonice as an impulse decision. But they also needed to get it to the market through out-of-home channels," said a consultant working with the brand. A dedicated sales force—known as the "impulse group"—succeeded in extending Liptonice into sports, entertainment, and travel channels. They spread the beverage into 50,000 outlets and gained the visibility and attention necessary to command shelf space and grow revenues and market share.

Representing Liptonice as the refreshment that "cools you down and picks you up" and linking it to sports and action gave the brand an energetic and youthful appeal. Starting in summer 1998, Liptonice sponsored annual beach volleyball events featuring tournament play and product giveaways. The combination of sun, surf, sweat, and skin featured in Liptonice commercials and promotions at sports events throughout the Netherlands. To keep sales going through the winter, Liptonice next began to sponsor ice-sporting events. Ice tea would thereafter be associated with "mountain madness" and the "snowboarder's heartbeat." A 62 percent volume growth in 1999, nearly matched again in 2000, reflected the success of these campaigns.

Exploiting New Channels: Cup-a-Soup

A large and growing range of out-of-home opportunities existed also for Cup-a-Soup. By tradition, soups in Holland are prepared by housewives for consumption at sit-down meals. With Cup-a-Soup's initial launch in the early 1970s, soup became an "instant product for individual consumption"—at any time of the day. Without much marketing directed at the consumer, out-of-home demand had nonetheless been growing 10 percent per year since 1993. The existing channels, however, were insufficient to reach the ambitious new goals set by the Foods business.

Cup-a-Office, as the prototype was dubbed inside VdBN, took an existing product and distributed it through new channels. At that time, Campbell Soup was experimenting with "Campbell's away from home" kiosks in railway stations, shopping malls, and other gathering spots. In the Foods group the idea arose of installing Cup-a-Soup vending machines in offices—making hot soup an alternative to tea or coffee.

Here, too, the outside-in perspective added new insights. An advertising manager reported: "We had originally positioned this as soup that you enjoy at home, with the product targeted at housewives. We realized that the product was certainly not the best soup out there. But it was better than coffee or tea." A colleague chimed in: "The second thing that happened was the realization that it's not only soup, it's also a snack. So you could have all kinds of Cup-a-Snacks to develop." A third added, "Because we put it down as a snack, from that moment on there was a complete new field. Your competitors were not other soups, they were Mars bars, coffee, and tea. It gave us a completely new field in which to maneuver."

As with Liptonice, an autonomous group was given responsibility for brand development, volume growth, and profit generation. This team had six to eight people including sales, marketing, and finance. They had a shared vision, stretch targets, and a passion to deliver. And positive results poured in. Cup-a-Soup dispensers appeared in small to medium offices, college dormitories, and high schools. By mid-1999 more than two thousand were installed with many more to follow in the next two years.

Tapping New Markets: Uno Noodles

Based partly on its history as a trading nation, Holland had plenty of Asian restaurants in the late 1990s, but no Asian fast food. Knowing the way noodles were consumed in Asia, marketers were convinced that they could be positioned in Holland as a snack food and become another platform for growth. The typical way Unilever developed this type of product was to involve a regional innovation center in testing the concept and its capacity for scale before moving ahead. Seeking to go to market more rapidly, an innovation team was formed in VdBN and given the license and leeway to develop the concept on its own.

But Asian noodles had several false starts. The recipe made for a good-tasting product, but the marketing concept ("Going Asian") and its positioning ("For people on the go") didn't catch on. The project was killed early 1998—at the cost of a year and a half of work. Still faith in the concept didn't go away. What kept it alive were intuition and daring, recalled a young marketeer:

> My colleagues dared to believe in my intuition. And I dared to listen to my own intuition. . . . You also need good analysis, etc., but only use them to feed your gut feeling—because in the end it is not only about one plus one is two. It's about what you believe in.

In early 1999 the Uno Noodles brand was launched with a new product and market definition—an "in-between meals snack" or a "quick and healthy meal." The initial marketing campaign targeted college students and featured free-spirited advertisements with attractive women in bikinis snacking away on noodles. Soon the product moved beyond the campus to factories, construction sites, and food carts and kiosks. The target market stretched to include blue-collar and office workers. The trade press credited Uno Noodles as the best product introduction of 1999. Over five and a half million noodle packages were sold that year.

Certainly the bold advertising added sex appeal to what everyone agreed wasn't the best-tasting meal in the VdBN portfolio. But in looking at their success factors, the team also stressed the importance of foresight, focus, and supportive leadership (Exhibit 9.2).

Promoting the Brands

A recipe for success was emerging in the Foods group.[3] A program review of the success of Cup-a-Soup in the office market emphasized the importance of interdisciplinary teamwork. As one of the

Exhibit 9.2 In Their Own Words:
Uno Noodles Success Factors

Foresight: Classic market research showed that noodles would not be a success in Holland. But we stuck to our conviction that "food travels" and that Europe would be the next frontier for consumption of noodles. Still, the intrinsic value of the product would have to be expressed in local terms.

Focus: Using the BCG matrix made it clear to everyone that noodles is a "star" category. We put a new organizational structure into place that allowed us to kick off the product, establish a new category, and quickly bring a new product to market.

Commitment: Project team had clear goals that were shared, the effort was fun and exciting. Our commitment was not only in words but also deeds. Resource issues were solved immediately. Negative profits were accepted for an initial three years.

Trust and Leadership: Trust from the troika was important in agreeing to the process and timing. The project leader was given space to take individual responsibility. More important, he allowed for chaos when necessary (to get higher-quality ideas) but also established order when the team needed it. He protected the team from others in the organization. He had credibility as a leader because we heard no "fake-certainties" from him.

leaders pointed out, "It was not just the idea but the execution that mattered." Through in-depth research by Palatex into the need-based appeal of snack foods, as well as surveys of current customers, the team acquired deeper knowledge of workplace hunger-and-eating habits and learned to translate that insight into winning brand promotions.

To capture busy office workers' attention and introduce them to the new image of Cup-a-Soup, for example, a series of "John the Manager" commercials promoted the brand with the image of a harried businessman who consumed soup on the move as a brief respite during a busy day. Refreshed and raring to go after his snack, John the Manager suffers some Chaplinesque calamity—in one, a heavy crate drops on him from above; in another, he bumps headfirst into a beam and falls on his bottom. These slapstick ads were the talk of television and won VdBN an award as Holland's most effective advertising campaign in 1999—plus their immediate effect of increasing Cup-a-Soup sales by 20 percent.

The award-winning John the Manager commercials and Liptonice promotions, along with sexy Uno Noodles advertisements, illustrated VdBN's growing capacity to connect to consumers and reach them with an appealing product and message. Nowhere was this more apparent than in the growth of Unox—the "cash cow" whose "mature" and "unexciting" brands were not considered candidates for investment.

Unox had earlier pushed for growth with "scratch quality" sauces and soups. The value proposition was that these would taste as good as those made at home and serve as their convenient replacement. The problem, noted Bauke Rouwers, was that "you just make good sauces without attention to the consumer." Then, in 1998, the Unox team held focus groups and home trials of several product variations. The scratch quality concept was first transformed into an elegant "soup in a glass" product line. Then it was extended to provide consumers with a full meal in a glass. Unox's "Chicken Tonight"—a mix of chicken and vegetables in a tangy sauce—could be served with pride at any Dutch dinner table.

On the promotion side, a variety of soups, sausages, and sauces were packaged in eye-catching orange boxes and sold at bargain prices. Retailers were supplied with an attractive display and offered incentives to promote the "orange boxes." Ten million were sold within a few weeks. Then a series of creative advertisements really boosted the business.

Unox brand manager Evert Bos (see spotlight) partnered with the advertising agency Lintas and formed a cross-company, multidisciplinary team, one that was, according to Bos, "truly connected, communicated feelings as well as knowledge, and developed shared brand ownership." To this point, Unox commercials and ads had featured a caring mother preparing soup for her children. Sensing a new market niche, Bos introduced the concept of the single-serving "one-person soup." His team then came up with an advertisement using the "Wonder Boys"—featuring a rock band breaking up and

Spotlight: Evert Bos

Evert Bos was a seven-year Unilever veteran who had always been in marketing, always working on the Unox brand, when the merger with VdBN took place. Says a colleague, "This guy, for me, is really the example of the artist. When you ask him to tell something about Unox, you could just sit down and listen to him for three hours, fascinated. He is one of those rare guys who really knows the brand, feels the brand, senses the brand, smells the brand."

Bos started with the Unox soup product, then became responsible for a few products under the Unox brand, then became the brand leader. "The shift in advertising of Unox was his genius," said a coworker. "Unox had always been a family brand, always very conventional. He knew that needed to change and succeeded in making it more alive."

then one of their fans, brokenhearted, finding comfort in a single serving of soup. The band became the talk of Holland—among young people—and one-person soup proved a winner.

The biggest splash came in 1999 with the annual January 1 dive of Hollanders into the icy waters of the North Sea. That year, and for every year thereafter, the swimmers—like the *Elfstedentocht* skaters two years earlier—wore the bright orange Unox hats passed out by VdBN employees on the scene. As with the skating, the dive received national media coverage. Tired, old Unox was now associated with an annual event that symbolized vigor, health, and fun. Commercials and an ad campaign that followed introduced a new logo for Unox—an orange-hatted penguin diving into an icy sea. It ranks today as one of the most recognized brand images in Holland.

Fun and Growth

Just as the Foods group promoted their brands with fun-loving images, they also shared fun and fellowship like a winning sports team. Marijn van Tiggelen, the smart and strong-minded young leader who had led the revolution in Foods, revealed a softer, fun-loving, community-oriented manner in leading free-spirited events for the Foods group. To celebrate year-end 1998, for instance, members of the business unit prepared a musical CD with songs that poked fun at their lifelines, chronicled further mishaps of John the Manager, and alluded to X-rated adventures with the Uno Noodles models. In 1999, putting the kitchen office to good use, the business unit prepared a banquet together. And in 2000, the Foods team put on a soap opera with Gunning driving the team into chaos.

On the more businesslike side of community building, Foods instituted the practice of taking time at the half-year point to reflect on the past six months and make commitments on targets for the second half of the year. This practice was institutionalized symbolically by handing out summer report cards to each group member.

The Foods business unit had achieved breakthrough results with 7 percent growth in 1998. And in 1999 it moved into double digits with 13 percent growth. The Foods story illustrates how a change in perspective about consumer needs and the future of food delivery opened up opportunities for growth. A fresh look at the product line, new food concepts and position, a stoking of competitive fires, and new ways of working all enabled the unit to grow from year to year.[4] Breakthroughs in the business unit continued through 2000 and on to this day.

Chapter 10

Growing a Brand

Fats

We are talking about two different games—a
market share game and a market growth game.
Growing our market share, being able to achieve
Index 100, is a game we learned to play. But that
has not solved the problem of how to grow new
markets.

—AJ van Triest, marketing director

Index 100 had directed the Fats business to grow its market share.
And beginning in 1997, through concerted effort, they had done
it—by maintaining prior year volume and thus increasing their
share of a shrinking market. But the singular focus on this short-
term goal had kept Fats from innovating and growing the top line.
"Index 100 was so absorbing—everybody was focused on it," rue-
fully recalled Jaap Kalma, a marketing manager. "But it was a dis-
traction from other things we were all struggling with. And we
weren't really able to crack the innovation part."

To make matters worse, the Fats practice of raising prices to
maintain profitability had actually helped to create a new class of
competitors. VdBN's higher-priced branded margarines, oils, and
spreads left an opening in the market that was being filled by lower
priced private labels. House brands—from both Dutch grocers and
international superstores coming into Holland—began to prolifer-
ate and threaten VdBN's hard-won market share gains.

False Steps: Cheese and Coffee Creamer

To "crack the innovation part," the Fats group first tried to build on its success with cheese spreads and move into the traditional brick cheese category. Begun before the merger of UVGN and VdBN, this effort accelerated when more emphasis was put on top-line growth. Sales director Leon Schoofs recalled:

> There was a clear attempt to redirect everything toward where there were potential volume growth and profit possibilities. But the Cheese unit was not a success, because we did not have a clue about that business—about cheese as a commodity. What we tried to do was to brand cheeses we purchased. And that was not something consumers were waiting for.

"As it happens often in our company, we wanted success too quickly and gave too little room for growth of the business," said a veteran of the Cheese unit. "We promised ourselves high volumes too quickly. It was a combination of too little knowledge of that market and lack of patience. If you want to start fighting in a different arena you must understand the rules of that arena to be successful. And we did not have the patience to wait and learn those lessons."

The Cheese unit had been managed by a category marketing team. Chastened by its failure, the Fats group set up its next venture—coffee creamer—to operate "like a separate company," with control over sourcing and distribution. The idea was to run it like a start-up—a business within a business with its own profit-and-loss accountability. This new structure emphasized entrepreneurship, built a business unit around a brand, and promised rewards for success. Yet, despite its innovative organization design (and partly because of it), many things began to go wrong. One problem was leadership of the unit. The unit leader had many of the aggressive and assertive qualities of the young people taking over in VdBN. But he operated like a lone wolf and lacked organizational know-how and savvy. As one manager recalled, "Coffee Creamer was a one-man operation. The leader got the space to do things and took advantage of this without informing or consulting others. He was just very solitary. That was a major problem."

Even worse, the unit leader neither sought nor received counsel from the leaders of the Fats group. A VdBN board member observed sadly, "We had one person in charge, and probably not the right person. But I don't think we helped him to think it through and really understand the business. We as leaders didn't realize that this man and this organization didn't fit together."

The Coffee Creamer unit's independence also proved a liability when it needed support from other functions in VdBN or had to coordinate work with external suppliers and distributors. "Strangely enough," said one team member, "we had no total overview of the project we were involved with."

Finally, the market spoke and, as an account manager heard it, "This one was mission impossible. After a half-year, we understood how our sourcing partner worked and what we could and couldn't do. But we also found out that coffee cream is of very little importance to a retailer. It's just a product he needs to have for his consumers but he won't invest in it. Still, our strategy stayed the same. We did not learn."

Changing Structure and Leadership

The Cheese unit was shut down, Coffee Creamer was folded back into the Fats business, and the entire unit was reorganized. The new organization separated value creation and value delivery—a structure that was proving successful in the Foods unit.

"We came up with the idea of separating value creation and value delivery in the organizational review team with the people from Foods," Conny Braams, then a category manager, recalled. "We recognized that you need people to develop the weapons and people to fight in the terrain." Finance director Janti Soeripto elaborated:

We needed people with the skills that could really take care of innovation for the longer term and for brand communication. And we needed people who were more business-oriented sitting closer to sales; launching new products, making promotions, making events, those kinds of concrete things focused on volume and profit. That's why we needed that split desperately.

In the new structure, the value creation side would take the long view and integrate R&D, innovation, and brand strategy and development. They would need "holistic consumer understanding" and be responsible for overall brand management. The value delivery side would have to connect supply and demand, handle day-to-day category and customer management, and be responsible for pricing, promotion, and channel- or customer-specific activities.

"Every theory book says structure should follow strategy," Braams noted, "but we waited too long to change the structure to make the strategy work." Next the team needed to do something about leadership. To this point, a single general manager had led the Fats unit—as was the norm throughout Unilever. Would something like the troika in Foods also work in the Fats business?

In May 1998 the Fats leaders held a hush-hush weekend meeting— without Neil Wickers, their then general manager (GM), who was overseas to scout out prospects for his next career assignment. At this point, the team was in conflict over its new structure and in turmoil about the GM's replacement: "The value delivery side started to blame the value creation part of the business that innovation was not there, that advertising was not good enough, and so on. The creation side started to blame the value delivery side for spending too much money on short-term, inefficient promotions."

Although not brewing a revolution—as had their counterparts in Foods—the members of the team spoke about the urgent need to change leadership and confronted each other over the way that they were (and were not) working together. After considerable talk, angry words, tears, and apologies, they came to a common resolve. They proposed, first, that the GM accelerate his move out of that role and, second, that he not be replaced by another Unilever high-potential or, for that matter, by anyone else. Instead of having a single GM, the Fats business would be run by a foursome: Leon Schoofs, the sales director, Janti Soeripto, the finance director, AJ van Triest, responsible for value creation, and Conny Braams (see spotlight), responsible for category management.

Spotlight: Fats Leadership Foursome

Aart-Jan (AJ) van Triest, a marathoner and student of business, had started working in VdBN in 1991. He worked as the marketing director of Fats, later assuming the role as head of value creation in Fats and in the European category team from 1998 to 2000. The results: "We are treating each other differently. We are more aware of the rules of engagement. When you create an environment where you are all on one side, you are able to get things on the table, even difficult issues, without harming people. What we achieved is less politics."

Leon Schoofs had joined VdBN Jurgens in 1988, after many years of experience in food businesses. Although the primary reason for his joining VdBN was his expertise in the cheese market, he stayed with the Fats business and joined the leadership team as the head of value delivery (sales). He came to life with the Big Night: "It wasn't the cooking book, it wasn't the promotion, it wasn't the display, it was the change in mindset that led to the great success of the campaign."

Conny Braams had worked four years at UVGN; she was a marketing manager at the time of the merger with VdBN. After the organization review in 1997 she became head of category management and joined the leadership team the next year. Her leadership truth: "To give individuals the feeling that they can make the difference is very stimulating and motivating."

Janti Soeripto joined the Fats leadership team as finance manager in the beginning of 1998, after six years in Singapore with another Unilever company. In March 2000, she took over as head of value creation. She encouraged self-entrepreneurship: "Let people make mistakes. We need to get out of the stable situation to grow."

Conny recalled the immediate benefits of the leadership change and some of the fallout:

> We decided that four of us would lead the business unit with one of us responsible for value creation, one for sales, one for finance, and one for category management. So we basically cut out one layer of management. We made it less hierarchical. And we would be more approachable. Every week there was an open meeting to discuss new ideas.
>
> What didn't work well in the beginning was that we each had our own agendas and didn't really have one voice. That was something we had to solve. People within our unit were tolerant, and their reaction was, "We know that a lot of things are changing, we understand that it takes time to become a real team." That was very encouraging.

Drawing on their experiences in the Ardennes and at the Learning Conferences, the new Fats leadership team talked openly about their conflicts and worked through a variety of interpersonal issues. One of the truly difficult issues on their agenda was figuring out how to grow their business. Janti recalled the breakthrough moment: "We needed to decide how to allocate resources and where to focus for growth. That's when we came up with the Blue Band seventy-five years idea."

Fighting the Competition: Reinventing Blue Band

The question that had been plaguing Fats was, How do you fight house brands?

"It took us half a year to develop a model," said Conny. "It is about cost cutting and price management in order to reduce the price that consumers pay and increase margins for the trade. That way there is less incentive for retailers to sell their own brands." The value delivery team concluded that this would shift market dynamics and enhance VdBN's fight for share. But what was the value proposition for consumers?

To answer that question, the value creation team reviewed a bit of history. Unilever's historic success in spreads, according to one team member, had been its science. Innovations such as soft margarine and low-calorie and water-free spreads had resulted from proprietary R&D and technology. Now all that was in the public domain—and in the products of competitors and house brands.

The other historic differentiator was the marketing genius of Jurgen Bol. In the 1970s, according to an old-hand marketeer, Bol had "branded the advertising" and created an "emotional bond" between Dutch consumers and Blue Band margarine. Blue Band had been, by all accounts, a powerhouse brand. The value creation team resolved that they would make it so again.

One problem was that, given changing consumer sentiments, Blue Band was at risk of being seen as simply a fat that you sometimes spread on bread—neither healthy nor distinctive. Accordingly, the value creation team revisited the category and the brand promise. AJ van Triest recalled:

> The interesting thing is, if you take away its categorization as a "fats" business, you could see a new use. We have a powerful brand, Blue Band, and Blue Band is all about giving mothers the best possible way to give their kids the best start of the day. The brand is incredibly strong. What could we do with that? Maybe we could focus on breakfast! And soon all sorts of other ideas poured out. There would be massive growth opportunities.

The idea that most appealed was to reinvent the brand as a healthy daily habit. In its rebranding and subsequent promotion, Blue Band promised to give children "a good start at morning breakfast" and "a welcome home at family dinner." The intent was to link the brand with "mothercare" in consumer's minds.

Another problem was to get the two sides of the business working together to deliver on this brand promise. Jaap Kalma, a key member of the launch team, noted, "We wanted to make the brand a daily habit. And every department, every person thought 'What can I do to make this brand a daily habit?' If you talk to the advertising agency, their focus was on this. And when you look at the sales department, they had exactly the same thing in mind. Total focus."

Value Delivery: The Big Night

The Blue Band promotion campaign was kicked off with two months of advertising about its 75th anniversary. Blue Band recipe cookbooks were distributed to bring the brand tangibly and visibly into every Dutch kitchen. "It all started with, 'Let's do a cookbook and give it out for free,'" said sales director Leon Schoofs. "But it's not a thousand books we were talking about—it was a million books. And that meant a budget of 5 million guilders—so, you see that it was a whole new game."

The game was to have consumers collect stamps from Blue Band packages to earn their "free" cookbook. Also, Blue Band cookbooks were not distributed in the typical way—through grocery stores. Instead they were made available at Blokker, a chain of stores offering gift items, cookware, toys, and other practical and fun family-oriented products. Connecting the promotion to this store, the team reasoned, would broaden Blue Band's mothercare image.

But the cookbooks were just a beginning to the 75th anniversary celebration. On the wind-and-rain-swept mountains of Scotland, the value delivery team had drafted and signed a pledge to "aggressively fight for every ton of volume to become an even more interdependent winning machine that works hard, plays hard, and has lots of fun" (Figure 10.1). They had carried this pledge into the 1999 Learning Conference, where they rallied their coworkers, and they carried it into the marketplace with the 1999 "Big Night."

The Big Night was an extension of the VdBN learning-conference-and-party concept—only this time aimed at connecting with customers.[1] Using their expertise from designing learning events in the company, Gerard Prins and his team orchestrated a program for fifty thousand retailers and grocers—ranging from distributors and store managers to shelf-stockers and checkout clerks—and their spouses and dates. The Big Night featured top-drawer entertainers, video

Figure 10.1 Fats Pledge for Volume Growth

presentations of commercials and two-way discussions about the Blue Band campaign, remarks by and Q&A with the Fats business leadership team, plus songs, drinks, and food aplenty.

Prins remembered the event fondly:

> The Blue Band seventy-five years event was . . . a turnaround in the Fats business. And it was an important moment for the leaders. Neil Wickers [former GM] was the captain but also a team player. He respected everybody and did not force things and took care of all sorts of troubles at executive level. We did not have to worry about that and could just go for operational excellence. So we did.

"We knew we needed people in the shops to support us," said Kalma, summing up the campaign and its impact. "So we thought we should do something for them—throw a thank-you party for all of the shop people in Holland!"

The program helped the Fats unit prove that they could break records and do the unthinkable. The dedicated team gave six months of their lives to live up to their dream. Their success was a major step in the mindset change within Fats. Its flagship brand was on the map again and customers were more interested in their "dull" category. And Blue Band increased its volume by double digits (from the pre-1997 rate of −7 percent all the way to +7 percent) and grew its market share from 19 to 25 percent.

Innovating in Europe

Unilever HQ took note of the Fats unit's success and decided in 1999 to create a pan-European organization for its Spreads and Cooking Category (SCC) with dotted line coordination in the hands of VdBN's chairman and the Fats unit. The goals of this structure were to reduce Unilever's overcapacity on the supply side and respond to consolidation of grocers.

SCC Europe adopted a number of VdBN practices.[2] The group undertook a strategic assessment, defined its intent, and set stretch targets—including a Europe-wide goal for achieving Index 100. SCC members also participated in two team-building outbreaks— one in the German forests and the other in the French Alps. With this new and diverse group of European managers, there was the predictable initial grumbling about camping out in tents and holding meetings via fishbowls. But, according to one attendee, "The whole journey was visionary, inspirational, and created an environment where people could accept the need for change." He went on:

> At the Munich airport, there was video footage of a daughter of the founding Van den Bergh family. She had a vision. "We wanted to make wholesome food for people. And, you know, my father created this business. He really cared for people. It is all about that legacy. Simon Van den Bergh drove this business with values about legacy and care."

In the end, the SCC category executives were convinced that they too needed to embrace their own legacy of growth.

The first results, in the form of volume growth and market share, appeared in late 1999 and early 2000. In addition to solidifying Blue Band's regional position, SCC introduced a cholesterol-reducing spread—Unilever's first entry into the arena of "functional food." As Janti recalled the innovation, "We had to pay attention to why the consumer was moving away from 'fats.' We had to offer products that could help consumers maintain a healthy diet." Becel "pro-activ" (as it was branded), started off badly with what Janti termed "terrifying ads so as to scare people into buying it." But then sales took off with a more upbeat campaign that reminded consumers that "a healthy heart keeps you fit for life."

Shortly thereafter, van Triest moved over to an SCC position and Schoofs retired, and the women were in charge. The foursome became a duo. Janti and Conny—two women from the ranks mentored into leadership—had the license to run the show. Janti reflected on her "current reality": "We still think we are producers of margarine, but we are also competing with producers of butter and olive oil. If your mindset is margarine, you do not feel real competition." To feel the competition, and get the business into the market growth game, Janti and Conny launched what one marketeer termed a "consumer-oriented strategy." One early win saw two young people take a line of prepared sandwiches to market using Unilever's Bertolli olive oil brand. A Europe-wide cheese-based spread was also launched at this time.

The success of these early efforts made it possible for the Fats team to see a clear path to top-line growth. They pledged that there would be 10 percent top-line growth in the Fats business—5 percent from existing brands and 5 percent from new categories. They hit the mark in 2002.

What motivated their drive to grow? Janti replied, "To show the skeptics that we could do it. To leave our own legacy of growth."

Chapter 11

Cascading Change

Uniquisine, Calvé, Royco, and Nassaukade

> I think with each event we improved in Van den
> Bergh. In July I went three days to Luxembourg
> with my whole group. I'm a firm believer of these
> kinds of events—really creating an environment of
> openness and challenge without any boundaries—
> just being yourself.
>
> —*Mick van Ettinger, director, Uniquisine*

The leaders responsible for business lines and sourcing units—
including several of the angry young men as well as some hard-bitten
old-timers—were the drivers of innovation down the organization
and in the factories. These tribe leaders, as they came to be called,
faced different business situations and worked with different kinds
of people. To cascade the transformation, they adapted the ideas
and techniques they had experienced and learned and put their personal stamp on local events.[1]

Turnaround of Uniquisine

Uniquisine lagged behind the transformation in the Foods business
until Mick van Ettinger, one of the young leaders in UVGN, came
to head up VdBN's small out-of-home business in April 1999. "My
boss basically said to me, 'Now run your own business unit and show
us what you can do,'" van Ettinger recalled. "That was all the brief-
ing I had. So when I came in here, I started listening to the people—
what their business was about."

Van Ettinger (see spotlight) found Uniquisine something of a backwater, out of the mainstream Foods business. Its products were pitched to institutional kitchens and restaurants, not the retail market, so it did not attract young, ambitious, or innovative marketers. "It was completely disconnected from the rest of VdBN," the marketer observed. "There was a big wall between Uniquisine and the rest of the company." To complicate its current reality: "We weren't growing fast enough. Profitability wasn't high enough. And people were all over the place. With a strategic review, the need for change became clear."

With a young captain at the helm, Uniquisine developed a new strategic intent. Now it would appeal directly to the dining-out consumer rather than serve only chefs and commercial kitchens with its sauces and soups. The aim was to get branded products on

Spotlight: Mick van Ettinger

"It was a dream come true" for Mick van Ettinger when he started at UVGN in 1993. He came in as assistant brand manager, then quickly moved up to become brand manager of a group of products. He was lucky to start with one of the best projects possible: Chicken Tonight, a product to be launched within three months because competition was coming in. "That was big fun, and to be honest, I didn't have a clue what I was doing," says van Ettinger reflecting on those days, "but I did it with all my drive and enthusiasm. We introduced a product and it was a big success."

In 1995 van Ettinger became responsible for the Royco brand and as senior brand manager his focus was Cup-a-Soup, including delisting all its extensions (such as Cup-a-Jus) and then changing its strategic intent from soup to snack. After the merger he started working in the Foods business unit as the account manager for Albert Heijn and was one of the eight young people to form the organizational review team. Two years later, in April 1999, he was appointed general manager of Uniquisine.

lunch tables and counters, and use the brands' reputation to add value to restaurant meals.

The strategic review had been performed with a small group, so now Mick focused on "the challenge of getting the rest of the organization on board." In July, the whole group went to Luxembourg for three days for a retreat to learn the strategy and "surface all the difficult issues."

"These were three days like the first team leaders' event in Ardennes," Mick recalled, "really creating an environment of openness and challenge without any boundaries—just being yourself." On mountain bikes and on foot, they moved from one awe-inspiring setting to another—fields and hilltops, a private castle in ruins, an ancient cloister—for reflection and sharing, deep discussion and moments of silence. Recalled event organizer Eric Jan de Rooij:

> They went to a cloister, by very beautiful fields . . . and spent one hour by themselves in silence. And then they came together and shared their experience and moved on again. We went canoeing, walked, and hiked. And every time it was changed, there were moments of talking and integration.

All these elements—the hard physical and mental work, intellectual and emotional engagement, plus the outdoor camping, skits, and song—combined to replicate the VdBN change process: a wake-up call, a look at current reality, visioning, and teaming all dramatized in exercises that Mick had learned at team leader events (see Exhibit 11.1).

Despite rain and cold, the Uniquisine team stayed dry and warm as they went about their business of mobilizing to reach their ambitious growth target—to triple sales by 2002. "In Scotland we learned that if you have rain, wind, and cold, people will not think," Mick explained. "They revert to a survival mode. So when we did Luxembourg, we took the learning from Scotland and had a contingency program: If it rains, where would we go? What if this or that happens?"

Exhibit 11.1   In Their Own Words:
van Ettinger on Uniquisine's Trip to Luxembourg

We started day one with facing current reality and a wake-up call. Inspired by what Tex had done at UVGN, it was a fake board proposal to sell off Uniquisine. In the train on the way to Luxembourg, half the group played the role of believers—they had to argue why this was the best proposal they had ever seen. And the other half were the cynics, arguing why this was an outrageous proposal.

Once we arrived to Luxembourg—in this beautiful surrounding—I told them the board proposal wasn't real, but that it was certainly a possibility in the near future. At the end of day one, we really had an emotional session where the current reality of Uniquisine seemed to emerge. Lots of emotional baggage carried from the past was openly discussed. The fog cleared.

Day two, the group was ready to start thinking where do we go from here? What are we good at? What should we focus on in the future? That's when we started crafting our vision to become experts in the out-of-home market selling the VdBN brands.

Day three was dedicated to aligning our personal visions with Uniquisine and reflecting on the question: "What should be my personal contribution?" We all had to write that on a piece of paper, put it in an envelope, and address it to ourselves—and three or four months later we all got that letter. We had done this in one of the learning conferences in VdBN and I found it worked really well. It's a great tool to keep the vision alive.

In just three days, the whole Uniquisine group was not only aligned behind ambitious goals but also had transformed their mindsets for quick action, as one product planner noted:

The strategy for 2002 would be to triple our current sales. So, you say, "Well, that's absolutely unreachable. It's far too high. You can dream of it, but you can never reach it." But now we have a new strategy and everybody is working to get there. You have to free your agenda to look at projects which were not formerly there. And, even if you did not consider it your job, you're going to think about it on Monday morning after the Luxembourg trip.

Execution moved ahead quickly, and a quick win came from offering the Unox brand soup in restaurants, complete with attractive promotional material, training for the restaurateur, and on-premises support—a high-quality soup that was "a total experience," in the words of one marketer.

Uniquisine achieved its operational targets in 1999 and in 2000. And, as the business developed, so did its people. Mick van Ettinger, too, experienced a breakthrough: "We pulled off a miracle here, I'm convinced. When I joined there were fifty people working here. Now I think there are some forty who are either new or have a different role. So pulling this off is something I really feel proud of."

Culture Change in Calvé

Ad van Oers (see spotlight), another of the young leaders from UVGN, took charge of Calvé, the unit manufacturing peanut butter and dressings, in 1999. There he found a factory still struggling with some of the old ways. "You had so little influence," recalled one veteran operator. "There were so many layers that you would not bother to give any opinion and, if you did, it would be used against you." Said another:

> Old Calvé was extremely hierarchical, more so than any other sourcing unit. Both in a positive and negative way. On the one hand a very protected family, on the other hand, everyone being mothered and fathered to such a degree that nobody took responsibility for the business.

Van Oers began a disciplined change effort—eliminating shift leaders, redesigning work, promoting self-managed teams, reenergizing TPM, and introducing a wide range of new practices. "There was a clear transformation model at Calvé," he recalled. "The seven steps of Kotter's model were in my mind.[2] Depending on the situation one or two of the things were more important."

Spotlight: Ad van Oers

Ad van Oers joined UVGN in 1991 as a shift leader and was among the first few Hans Synhaeve picked to help run the meat factory, which was losing more than half a million guilders a week. van Oers and Alwin Maaskant were given charge of the factory, each accountable for one of the major production lines. After the merger in 1997, Alwin moved to a new assignment in Germany. Ad was in charge of the meat factory.

In 1999 Ad was appointed as plant manager to Calvé, the manufacturer of dressings, mayonnaise, and peanut butter, which was in serious need of a turnaround. "I told the management team of Calvé, when I came in, that they were a bunch of criminals: they were responsible for 160 people, for 160 families," recalled Ad. Now, he says, "The biggest joy for me is to see people living up again now and taking initiative. One of the major success factors was that you create space, room for people to develop and to run the business like they own it."

But the situation facing Ad and his team was tricky. Calvé had already been through several rounds of restructuring—layoffs, delayering, shutting down its snack peanut business—and had even begun hosting its own learning conferences. As one team member put it, "We got halfway up the mountain and concluded that we were running in circles." In some respects, Ad's team found themselves in the same disconnected place as VdBN's board had been in Antwerp. "It was almost as if they did everything according to the textbook," said one observer, "but forgot one vital thing—to put the bits back together again."

To help to reconnect people, Ad recalled how Hans Synhaeve and Tex had walked the factory floor when they took charge at Unox. He did the same at Calvé. Said Albert Desaunois, the union representative:

The new guy who came in actually moved his office on the shop floor, came out of the ivory tower, and spent all his time walking around on the shop floor. So he made a big effort to reconnect. And then we finally started to see some results.

Through walks on the factory floor, and his own personal reflection, Ad developed a personal insight to add to his change model: "You should really *live* the change. I believe that people who live the change will succeed." He and his team took to heart the Gandhian principle—"Be the change you want to see in the world"—and carried it with them in their day-to-day dealings. Ad and his management team were close by, in the factory instead of their offices—more accessible and more open than the "old Calvé" management.

Slowly and surely team leaders and members sensed openness, trust, and space in the work environment. A new culture began to emerge:

- *From Operator A:* It's a different company than five years ago. I feel much closer to management. I am motivated to work faster and better. I can act on my own initiative and get quick feedback. We produce more with fewer people. The workload is higher and we have less time for other stuff that was fun. But I get more satisfaction from what I do. I like having more responsibility.

- *From Operator B:* Because trust is given, people initiate their own actions. I think this a major cultural transformation. People speak more honestly and openly to each other than five years ago—no longer secretly in the coffee break, but in the office or in meetings where there are twenty people. People have gained a lot of courage.

The sense of reconnection and trust had tangible benefits in Calvé. Absence rates due to illness, formerly a problem in the factory, were at a record low in 1999—the best in Unilever. And, as happened in the Fats unit, Calvé began to reconnect to other parts of Van den Bergh. Said Desaunois, the union rep, "People realized, 'We have to produce at low cost so that our colleagues in Rotterdam can sell our stuff. That is our bread.' There is now awareness of the fact that it is not only about Calvé, it is also about marketing, sales, and advertising. We need each other."

The once-languishing sourcing unit also began to reconnect with its consumers. Soon a Calvé advertising campaign, featuring a young boy kicking a football and enjoying Calvé peanut butter, won the company an advertising award and revived the brand in the marketplace. Later, the youngster from the advertisement kicked footballs into the audience during the annual Learning Conference and starred at the Fats unit's Big Night. He was seen as a winner and so now was Calvé.

Keeping It Simple at Royco

The success of Cup-a-Soup created demand for volume and an opportunity for growth for its sourcing unit, Royco. When Roef van Duin, another of the young leaders from UVGN, was appointed as Royco's plant manager in spring 1998, he brought a passion for business and personal growth to his new unit. "If you ask me what is important or what we are here for," van Duin remarked, "I would say it's for building people. Results will follow, I am sure."

Roef (see spotlight) also had a distinctive view on how to grow a business: "Growth is not about money, it is about soul work." Not surprisingly, Covey training and community building figured large in the change program at Royco. And their big value, said a colleague, was the "positive impact on the culture."

Change at Royco extended beyond people development; there were layoffs and delayering, stretch targets and TPM, and a number of other management innovations, including team- and community-building efforts. But the way these changes were introduced, and the way the factory was managed, was kept simple—and on a human scale. "Because we are small, we had to do things very efficiently,"

Spotlight: Roef van Duin

Roef Van Duin joined UVGN in 1993 as a shift leader and was handpicked by Hans and Tex to become the production manager in 1995 in the sauce factory. Later, he was given full authority as well as profit-and-loss accountability. "Roef was extremely inexperienced at that time and very young but very smart," recalled Tex. "We appointed him, and that was nothing else but a gamble. And when we gave Roef the job he lived up to the expectations."

After a year and a half as sauce factory plant manager, he moved in 1998 to lead yet a bigger factory, Royco in Utrecht, the manufacturer of Cup-a-Soup. "He is a real visionary leader," says Royco's HR manager. "We have a leader who supports team building and investing in people. We worked on our three-year vision as a team. We as a team have values and beliefs, we listen to each other, and we have respect for the differences. And there are lot of results: Volume is up, costs are down, operational efficiency is 20 percent higher."

Roef remarked. "The first year was very much about making choices: We do this and we do not do that." Ankie van Lindt, the Royco team trainer, elaborated:

> Our idea is to be consequential, choose what you choose, have a vision and work at it all the time—every day. For example, we have every morning a meeting about the last twenty-four hours and the next twenty-four hours. We say it is not bad to make a mistake. But talk about it. Put it on paper; do not let it go. This is how we run the factory.

The Royco unit held various outdoor events from 1998 through 2000. A typical scenario would involve the whole factory in two days of team training. In their natural work groups, people would participate in exercises such as apple picking or a Lego building-block competition, and then use the experience to discuss how they worked together in the factory.

"It was simple, inexpensive," recalled Ankie. "It was talking about 'How do we work together?' 'What is your role as a team leader?' 'What is your vision of things?'" She added, "You can't only have people with a passion for change. It's not just beautiful theories about learning and organization change. It's also thinking about the basics. Focus on normal things."

Returns and Results

All the outbreaks and team building in the sourcing units were not ends in themselves. On the contrary, they had always been coupled with TPM training and aimed at improving results.[3]

A look at results for the sourcing units overall shows the scale of performance improvements. The metrics of success in the Fats and Foods business were double-digit top-line and volume growth. The latter was evident in the success of factories: Royco grew its volume by over 30 percent from 1995 through 1999, and Unox and Calvé grew their volume by roughly 10 percent. A more definitive indicator of success was operating efficiencies, as shown in Table 11.1.

At Unox, efficiency increased from 55 percent to 80 percent from 1995 to 1999. Nassaukade and Calvé, which had started their transformations in 1997, also increased their efficiencies by one-third or more. Though pressed to keep up with the demand for Cup-a-Soup, Royco nevertheless increased efficiency by some 6 percent. With a mix of staff reductions—through layoffs, delayering, and restructuring—and productivity improvements, costs went from 252 to 148 million guilders—a cost improvement of 41 percent. The bulk of the improvement came in the first two years, reaching 168 million guilders in 1997.

Table 11.1 Operational Efficiencies at VdBN Sourcing Units

	Royco	Calvé	Nassaukade	Unox
1995	70	50	60	55
1999	75	70	80	80

In the Nassaukade margarine factory TPM and other improvement projects led to considerable savings while reducing toxic waste levels significantly (see Table 11.2). These results funded the extraordinary trip to the Sinai, one that would allow production workers to grow personally and build yet a stronger community.

A Trip to the Sinai

At the other end of the spectrum from Royco's simple and inexpensive way was the team-building program at the Nassaukade led by a gray, grizzled, independent-minded department head named Geert Maassen (see spotlight).

The idea of teamwork was not a new idea for the Nassaukade production department Centrale Afdeling (CA) at the time of the Ardennes. Maassen had started teamwork on his own in 1995. By late 1997, he had left his management post to coach a CA team that aspired to become a self-managing group.

Maassen came alive with the mix of activity, reflection, nature, and fresh air in the Ardennes. As a follow-up, he suggested a sailing

Table 11.2 Return on Investments of Improvement Projects in Centrale Afdeling

Estimated total costs (in guilders): 200,000

Estimated total returns (in guilders): 2,000,000

Twenty-five people instead of thirty-two; delegating more responsibility to the workers:	2 million guilders per year through improvement projects (in guilders):	
	Autoplanner	468,000
Overtime, work schedule	Decrease in oil loss	40,000
Vacation planning	Decrease	
Production planning	ingredients loss	410,000
Technical maintenance	Savings from waste	
Improvement projects	water	290,000
Supplier relations	Operational efficiencies	800,000+

> ### Spotlight: Geert Maassen
>
> Nassaukade veteran and teamwork pioneer Geert Maassen was head of the production department at the time of the UVGN-VdBN merger. Maassen took his team-building efforts to a new level, with a vision to deliver top results as a self-managing team. "Everybody in the factory wants to work in our group," said one of the team leaders coached by Maassen. "He has completely changed into an eager and proactive person," remarked another colleague.
>
> Maassen also pioneered the learning history effort by producing a very detailed account of his team-building efforts from 1995 to 2000 and outlining the twenty-some important lessons they learned along the way. He offered the book co-created by all the members of his department as a farewell gift and thank-you to Tex.

trip on the clipper ship *Johanna* for team building across the three CA shifts. The team leaders liked the idea and handled the logistics—food, transport, insurance, accommodations, and so on—with no assigned leaders. During the sail, assignments were introduced, worked out, and evaluated by the teams themselves. Shift leaders served as coaches and discussion leaders. They also recorded the event. Their reports, illustrated with personal notes and photographs, were sent to the management board as testimony to the progress made in team building. Maassen himself made a presentation to a post-Ardennes meeting of all VdBN team leaders in fall 1998 where he showed how, in his experience, "teams make a difference."

On their return from Scotland in 1999, the CA team leaders vowed to recreate their experience for everyone in their unit, with even more mystery and drama. That spring, CA employees were told to bring clothes for warm weather and to be prepared to travel by air to an unknown destination. One worker recalled, "We started to speculate on where we were headed and it kept us busy before we got onto that bus." Added another, "I was in the night shift but I thought it's OK, I will sleep the whole day. But I got no sleep at all; I was just too excited."

The Sinai desert was chosen as the venue because it presented a totally different context—a place nobody had been before and likely nobody would return to again—a once-in-a-lifetime experience. As Maassen recalled it:

> It came up as I was brainstorming with Eric Jan [of MLT travel] about where we should go. Something memorable needed to happen. What one can do there, is not possible anywhere else. It is indescribable how the environment impacts you. Something you cannot achieve at the beach in Noordwijk [a Dutch beach resort] or even in the Ardennes. The space and the silence made a great and unforgettable experience.

Physical exertion would be part of the trip—reasonable but tough walking in the desert, high temperatures, living out of tents. So would emotions and time for reflection. An FCE facilitator, Adriaan Bertens, stressed the importance of "not just sharing ideas and experiences but rather 'going inside' and speaking from a 'deep place.'" Each day, very difficult and vulnerable conversations took place in the desert oases. "We were there without our masks," said one worker. "We talked utterly openly and freely with each other."

There are no statistics by which to gauge how much a stronger connection between the three shifts affected productivity in CA. But testimonials abound. "I do not really know if you have to go that far away to be open to each other," the works council representative said, "but Sinai really had a great impact in the change process. I think that it has to do with dealing with each other in a different manner. You showed yourself and then you also got a lot back."

Maassen had this to say about the overall results. "The sickness rate is low in our group, everybody wants to work in CA. And we really saved lots of money, a couple of millions in a couple of years. All this by investing in people."

What did the investments in people produce? Listen to this one "shy bird":

If you see how we all have changed! I used to be a silent, shy bird; now I am learning to use my mouth. You also see it in the way people have started to think along on the shop floor. Everybody is involved with what is going on. But also in small stuff, like putting paper in the printer or wiping the floor. It has become like it's our own company.

When they came back from the Sinai, the CA team compiled another "book" to document their experiences in team building, both at the plant and in the desert. And they proudly showed a video of the Sinai trip to the management board.

The wheels started turning and talk began about the value of capturing the learnings in all of VdBN, about taking all the team leaders to the desert, and about Tex's impending departure and replacement. The idea was set: To go to the desert and reflect back on what happened and what could be learned.

Part V

Transfer

Chapter 12

To the Desert

If you do not set ambitious goals you will not touch
upon the heart. You will step into a managing
mode. If you double your targets, you mobilize the
company. People have to reinvent themselves to
get there.

—*Tex Gunning*

Old and young, women and men are weeping quietly, and Tex's
voice is barely audible, muffled by tears: "That's it, I am gone now."

The 180 VdBN team leaders are in Ed Deir—a Nabataean
monastery built into an immense cliff face in Petra, Jordan. The
drama of VdBN's transformation is at its peak. This is the final
scene. After four days in the desert of Wadi Rum, reflecting on the
past five years they have worked together, the leaders of the business are gathered in this sacred place to say good-bye to their leader.

The departing chairman and his "tribe leaders" (the six now leading the different units of the business) are standing in a small elevated
chamber. The little light penetrating into the monastery is focused
on them. The tribe leaders are joined in a semicircle behind their
leader, facing the audience. The acoustics in the dark, close space are
such that you can hear every breath. And Tex continues: "I am leaving, you can do it. But you have to reinvent yourselves. . . ."

Gunning steps down after what seems like endless applause,
passing the torch to his successor, Anthonie Stal. The two keep on
hugging each other, through tears and cheers. "This was not in the
script," Karen Ayas made a note to herself. "There was absolutely

no way of predicting how this scene would play out. Until the last minute, we were not even sure that the new chairman would be there. And I am not sure that there ever *was* a script."

But no question that this scene had been carefully staged. Many hours had gone into the meticulous design of this event in Jordan, seeking to create, scene by scene, just the right setting and circumstances.

Wake-Up Call III

The idea guiding the preparations for the team leaders' trip to the Jordanian desert and the Learning Conference 2000 to follow it was the necessity of achieving revolutionary growth. In sounding his third wake-up call in five years, Gunning asked his team to embrace "new economy" aspirations and to reinvent themselves.

"How is the business world going to look in the next five to ten years?" he challenged the team leaders to ask themselves. "If you truly believe that we are in a new economy, then that is what we should be thinking about in Unilever. If we want to grow Unilever, we have to reinvent ourselves."

In the last five years, VdBN had transformed itself from a no-growth business to one that had achieved at least modest gains in some areas—and remarkable results in others. Now they had to accelerate the growth. How could they do the next reinvention? Gunning made an analogy to the Olympics:

> Many people are extremely proud when they qualify for the Olympics. We've done that. But there are some people who go to the Olympics to win gold. And you know that there is a huge difference between qualifying and winning gold. It means you've got to commit yourself, it means hard training. We're qualified but now we say, "We will be the best in the world. We will achieve gold."

The company would have to go into analysis again. "You've got to commit yourself to reflect on what went right and what went wrong. It will take commitment to persevere. And it will be an in-tellectual challenge to see what you can do differently than in the past. But you've got to go through the analysis. . . . Because if you allow yourself to continue as you are, results will slowly slide away."

It was a wake-up call all right, but quite different from the first two. This time Gunning was leaving, not arriving on the scene. VdBN was in no evident crisis. It was a beacon of growth in Uni-lever in the midst of a shifting scene.

A Shifting Scene

Unilever had completed its reorganization in Europe in late 1999, linking VdBN's Fats business unit with related businesses in other countries under the mantle of the Spreads and Cooking category (SCC). With this reorganization, the chairman of VdBN assumed dotted-line responsibility for the SCC category, and the chairs of other countries would have some say in VdBN's Foods businesses.

This raised key questions about executive authority, business unit autonomy, and in general how to do business in a restructured Europe. "I do not think there is as much space and freedom to do your own thing," was the way one of the tribe leaders summed it up. "We have had the philosophy of managing our budgets to stretch targets," said another. "We reinvested in people and in systems to grow the business. What is happening now is that we are managing our results by cutting down our capabilities."

In addition to reorganizing, Unilever had instituted across-the-board cost cutting in light of its slump in the market. That, plus the fact that Hans Synhaeve had accepted a new position in Unilever and that Gunning would soon be leaving for his next post, caused concern and restlessness within VdBN. "In the past," a tribe leader observed, "we said that during peacetime, you have to practice for war. We continuously pushed. Some new leaders think that we do not have to do more training. They're wrong!" Said another tribe leader: "You need a very ambitious purpose. If you do not have that, people will fall back into the behavior of the old culture." In preparation for the team leaders' event in Jordan to be held in February 2000, Gunning tuned in to these tensions to set the stage for a new wake-up call: "I see the slipping too. I think it has partly to do with the fact that we achieved what we set out to do. Now we have to create the next level of inspiration and aspiration."

To move forward, he said, they would begin by looking back:

> Look at the principles that guided us this far. First, we always made decisions as if it was our own business. Second, everything we did was around people: Finding people, empowering people, encouraging people, inspiring people, and helping people. The old culture of VdBN was about brands, not about people. And I don't want the old culture creeping back in.

Journey to the Past

The time had come to document the transformation of VdBN over the last five years. The formal process of preparing a "learning history" was assigned to the authors and a team of select VdBN leaders.[1] Its aims were to identify key transforming events, locate their meaning and significance, and assess their impact on employees and the business (see Appendix 2.)

Eventually, everyone from top to bottom in the company would be involved in analyzing events and detailing the lessons learned. In Jordan the team leaders would weave through time and space to look at VdBN's past and future—its accomplishments from 1995 to 1999, and the challenges that lay ahead. With the aim of looking backward and striving forward, the slogan created for this physical and metaphorical journey was "Learning from the Past to Compete for the Future."

The team leaders' journey through time began in Holland with the challenge to create a timeline of key events for themselves and their businesses. A prework assignment stimulated thinking:

> To create our next breakthrough, we need to learn from the last five years. Remember where we were five years ago. We knew we had to

grow but didn't know how. Year one, nothing happened. Year two, the first 2 percent came out. Year three, 4 percent came out. And so on. Some units turned around faster than others. Some units started later but then went faster.

So what can we learn? What are the key events and milestones of the last five years? What are the learnings? What were really significant breakthroughs for our business unit? And for me as a leader: What did I learn? What experience in the last five years can I bring forward to help achieve the next breakthrough?

"We were very enthusiastic because we had to do some work in advance," said a safety manager, "both visioning and learning from the past. First think of what you want to do in the future, then think about your learnings from the past. If you start forgetting the past, you will fall back into your old habits or make the same mistakes."

The trip to the desert began with a flight to Jerusalem and a tour through the Jewish, Christian, and Muslim quarters of that holy city. What better way for the team leaders to prepare to learn from history than to immerse themselves in it and in all of its complexities and quandaries? The symbolic start of their storytelling was a bus stop alongside the Dead Sea. All wearing their orange Unox hats, the 180 team leaders jumped into the salty water—a reenactment of the revival of Unox in the historic 1997 dive-into-the-sea after the Dutch skating holiday.

Later, under the starry desert sky, they set up tents in a Bedouin campsite in the desert of Wadi Rum to spend the night. Amid the music, and food, and fun, the exhausted team leaders were keenly aware that a challenging agenda awaited them in the morning: to develop their lessons learned from their timelines and put them to use going forward. They would start with visioning—the idea was to think like revolutionaries.[7] As Cumming had put it:

The exponential change in the outside world dictates that we will have to create a revolution in our Van den Bergh/Unilever world. The New Economy will have a very significant effect on our lives and our business.

Moving from 80 percent to 90 percent operational efficiency does not reflect New Economy values and beliefs. Owning your own factory, selling your services, inventing new technology, efficiencies of 120 percent—that's the New Economy. The visioning is about business but it is also about us—what do we want, how do we want to live our lives?

For the next three days, surrounded by the stark beauty and historic significance of this desert place—and living as close to nature as a Bedouin tribe—the team leaders individually and together explored their history, lessons learned, and needed plans and actions (see Exhibit 12.1). They found many similarities and some differences in their history lines and in their interpretation of events.

What they found in common was that most had experienced breakthroughs—in their business and in their personal lives. And many realized that the journey to this time, in this desert, had been not just physical but intellectual and emotional—and some would say spiritual. As one team leader reflected:

My major breakthrough was to experience the meaning of being a leader. The fact that it is intellectual, emotional, physical, and spiritual. That I am a leader twenty-four hours a day. That it is fun but also difficult to be consequential and sharp at all levels and at all times.

And to realize that reflection is necessary to grow as a leader.

Talking quietly and arguing passionately, sometimes laughing, sometimes tearful, the various "tribes" created banners that highlighted their most meaningful experiences from 1995 to 2000. At the end of the day, around a roaring campfire, they showed one another their banners and explored the significance of what they had done. Everyone understood that they were not only learning from history, they were making it.

"Some things after a while seem quite natural and become 'the way we do things around here,'" observed a plant manager:

Exhibit 12.1 In Their Own Words:
Team Leaders in Jordan

Day 1. The chairman sets the stage by addressing the question why we are here. After half a day of experiencing Jerusalem, we head south. We stop for a dive into the Dead Sea and continue until we reach the border into Jordan. Once we cross the border the tribes are separated into different campsites. After two hours of bumpy Jeep ride in the dark, we end up in a Bedouin campsite in the desert. Tents are set up; there is food and a campfire. It is a beautiful night but we are all exhausted and go to sleep.

Day 2. We wake up with the sounds of camels. We are in the middle of this immense desert with pink sand and multicolor rocks. We have about an hour camel ride (camels are the most relaxed animals, and they seem to be in tune with the majestic scenery). As we continue our ride, other groups of camels appear in the horizon, each coming from a different direction. We form a big circle and the tribes are called upon to unite for their new mission. We start a long "process" day, most of the day engaged in reflective conversations perched on rocks.

We spend the morning on visioning and the afternoon discussing at a very deep level what had been significant in the past five years, walking through the years. In preparation for the event, team leaders had been asked to reflect on their individual history, the major breakthroughs and the significant moments in the past five years. Now they construct their learning history as a unit. At the end of the day, we have collective sharing around a huge fire. We form a big circle with each tribe holding their banners marked with years and the most significant learnings. We walk back in pairs to our campsites in the dark, sharing personal visions this time. Conversations around the business and personal stories continue into the night.

Day 3. A whole day of riding on bumpy roads in Jeeps. Each time we stop, people swap Jeeps and continue to share their learnings from the previous day. The last stretch of the ride is gripping. At the end of the day, just as it gets dark, we reach our campsite; all tribes now united in one spectacular site. The community feeling is enhanced by a huge campfire in the middle and caves surrounding us.

Day 4. We leave the campsite early morning for a five-hour hike to Petra. This is a scenic trail with quite a few dangerous passages leading to the monastery on top of the mountain. All make it to the monastery for the final scene: the passing of the torch.

It is not obvious that you are doing things in a different way unless you deliberately look back. For new people coming in, who have not been part of the process, some of the learnings are not so obvious. You have to remember and share. Otherwise, you will make the same mistakes again.

Back to the Future

The process of visioning in the Jordanian desert helped the VdBN team leaders "see" their desires, what was important to them, individually and collectively, and what they were willing to bring into being. Knowing, articulating, and sharing what mattered to them would help to reawaken the company to its latest challenge. "Revolutionary growth," it was agreed, would require "reinvention of the old business units—at the level of people's values and beliefs." Hans Cornuit explained:

> We need to know what worked well and understand our organizational histories. What took each unit from a period of no growth to a time of growth? . . . All eighteen hundred Van den Bergh people need to be involved in capturing, developing, and sharing the history.

The team leaders would take their insights and learnings from the desert back to the organization. Having the team leaders travel afar to talk business, share personal stories, and then return to reenact the experience for the entire organization had become a standard practice for VdBN since the 180 leaders took charge in 1998. What was new in 2000 was the use of the learning history method to help the team leaders document and evaluate their experiences and apply their learning to their agenda of growth. "This is the first time we are really digging into the past," observed a VdBN team leader. "This is the kind of dialogue we hope to have over the next few months. It's a way of running the business."

The team leaders' job was to engage eighteen hundred others in reviewing past experiences and identifying their visions for the future. But visions are often difficult to speak about because of the gap between what you desire and the present situation. The creative tension between vision and current reality had been palpable in Jordan—the uncomfortable sense of "given where we are, how do we get to where we need to be?" Recalled Anthonie Stal, the incoming chairman:

> I will never forget that Tuesday when we sat with tribe leaders and with the doubts that were around the table—"How are we going to do this?" And we went from knowing it had to be done to believing it can be done and then getting it done. That all happened within four, five days. That's when I saw the value of doing an event like this with the leadership group. You actually can then take it to the Learning Conference with the eighteen hundred and get all those people on board.

Learning Conference 2000

Tears and cheers accompanied Tex Gunning's good-bye to all employees and Anthonie Stal's arrival as chairman at the Learning Conference the week after the team leaders were back from the desert. "I have never seen anything so emotional," said a promotion manager.

After the tears and cheers, every VdBN employee—board members, team leaders, line workers, and office staff—participated in the visioning process the team leaders had experienced in Jordan. Then they shared their five-year history lines and listened intently as their teammates did the same. Each team constructed its own timeline and prepared a learning history book detailing their stories of personal and business breakthroughs—and their visions for their future.

Both outgoing and incoming chairmen went around and talked with the teams as they prepared their visions and learning history books. Their conversations with each of the units were projected through televisions around the meeting hall and Tex said his good-byes one-by-one and en masse.

A new leader was in charge. Would VdBN continue to transform itself? A laboratory worker spoke for most of the eighteen hundred at the closing scene:

> Well, think of it this way. You are running in the marathon and you have reached the thirty-fifth kilometer. And they tell you to stop. You have another seven kilometers and you know you can do it. If the public is no longer with you—and there is nobody to cheer or applaud—you would continue, wouldn't you?

Chapter 13

The Legacy of Growth

What frightens me is that you develop a culture
that is focused specifically around the leader. And
as soon as that leader leaves there is no legacy that
can be carried on by the people who remain.

—*Former general manager, Foods*

Could VdBN carry on its legacy of growth? Would the tribe leaders
live up to their promise and lead another revolution? With the passing of the torch at Petra, the burning question in VdBN was
whether or not the transformational agenda could be sustained.

At the time, there were different answers to this question. Some
believed the legacy of growth had been institutionalized.[1] The company physician Alex Korbee said, "The process as a whole is not
going to stop. It will go further and people will be even more involved. That is what I hear in the factory, in the canteen, or when
I talk to people." Others were less sanguine. "It can slide back," said
one of the tribe leaders. "The way we bettered the organization was
by developing people. That stopped at a certain moment . . . at least
that is the impression I have." But the great majority were simply
uncertain. As a distribution manager put it, "One issue to consider
is staff turnover. In a management team you need a balance between people who want to move on in their careers and people who
want to stay here. When people leave, they take their experience
with them."

The New Leader's Dilemma

It's never easy to follow a charismatic leader, particularly one that issues a daunting challenge for yet another round of revolutionary growth. From the start, Anthonie Stal encountered a tough, we'll-show-you-how-we-do-things attitude in VdBN. (Ironically, this was the same attitude that had greeted Gunning three and a half years earlier.) Hans Cornuit described the current mood as follows:

> In June 2000, we had the fifty or sixty members of the works council together to talk about what was happening. What came out of the conversation was "No one can get us back to where we were. A new leader will have to adjust himself to the way we do business."
>
> I must say that this is what I would expect to hear from senior managers, but not from the works council.

The attitude among senior managers was frosty as well. For one thing, cost-cutting had continued through 2000 throughout Unilever. Needing funds to grow their top lines, VdBN leaders were irked to have to cut back as much as other Unilever businesses that were not growing at all. And though Stal had an accomplished track record, he shared no history with the VdBN leaders and thus could not inherit their loyalty.

The fallout was most pronounced among the young leaders who had been personally groomed by their former chairman. "We, the young leaders, were all connected to Tex, and therefore connected to each other," explained one, "but when he left, the bonds among us didn't stay so strong." As a result, these leaders of the business and sourcing units, already protective of their shrinking budgets, began to focus more on their individual areas of responsibility and less on VdBN overall.

Furthermore, Anthonie himself wasn't comfortable with the scale and costs of the activities that had been staged at VdBN in the name of team and community building. And, quite naturally, he wanted to put his own leadership imprint on the company. Much

to the consternation of the VdBN team leaders, their 2001 outbreak was canceled. So was the upcoming all-company Learning
Conference. Attention turned instead to handling the integration
of a major corporate acquisition.

A Game-Changing Merger

Another, and more significant, factor upsetting VdBN's near-term
growth agenda was Unilever's acquisition of America-based Best-
Foods in 2000. With its stock price still down, the parent company
looked to grow via acquisition of key BestFoods brands including
Knorr (soups and sauces), Hellmann's (mayonnaise and spreads),
and Wishbone (dressings). That same year, Unilever also purchased
two additional companies: Ben & Jerry's ice cream and Slim-Fast,
the diet food maker—an ironic pairing. The BestFoods deal would
change the organizational profile and product mix of VdBN—and
its corporate identity. The combined company would be called
Unilever BestFoods Nederland (UBF-NL).

Throughout the fall of 2000, while challenged to establish himself with VdBN's leadership group, Stal was consumed with work on
transition teams merging the two companies' European organizations and product lines. Unilever, in turn, announced a "game changing" plan to focus primarily on global brands and eliminate many
local offerings. The effect on VdBN was substantial:

- Knorr, the soup brand of BestFoods, would replace Unox
  soups.
- Royco, maker of dry soups and sauces, would be sold.
- The Fats business would be fully integrated into UBF Europe.

By the beginning of 2001, Stal had integrated the two product
lines in Europe and the two country businesses in Holland, and a
whole new management board including BestFoods managers was
in place. Only two former VdBN business unit leaders were part of
the new board, now called the "leadership team."

With the new organization and its leadership sorted out, Anthonie found his stride. He undertook team building with his board in early 2001 and took team leaders from the pan-European Spreads and Cooking Category (SCC) on an outbreak to his homeland, the Andalucia region of Spain.

And what happened to the young leaders? By this time, AJ, the former tribe leader in Fats, had taken an assignment in SCC—a promotion. Hans Cornuit left Unilever to head HR at another Dutch company. Roef, whose Royco factory was to be sold, would take over the factory in Nassaukade—now the sourcing unit for all of Europe. And by mid-2001, Marijn, Mick, and Ad—tribe leaders of Foods, Uniquisine, and Calvé respectively—all took other assignments within Unilever.

The More Things Change . . .

By the fall of 2002, UBF-NL had come into its own and started putting its own stamp on the VdBN legacy of growth. One Monday in September, for example, the UBF-NL headquarters in Nassaukade buzzed with an excitement not unlike years prior—about a hundred people had just returned from a memorable event dubbed the "pioneer days." An internal team had designed and facilitated the three-day event to launch the UBF strategic program for the Netherlands. Though they had traveled no further than their homeland, they had expanded the scope of the gathering to include time not just for their business agenda but also to build a small stadium and soccer field for children in a poor neighborhood. The inauguration of the stadium—a soccer game with the pioneers playing alongside the neighborhood kids—had been the grand finale of the outing.

"By now," said Gerard Prins in early 2003, "there are just a handful of us remaining here at UBF. We have adapted to a new and different leadership style." But, even so, many of the former chairman's themes and priorities remain alive and well. Roef, for instance, has set a stretch goal of doubling volumes in Nassaukade by

2004. Team building and TPM continue, and many work units still have outbreaks and learning gatherings, albeit on a smaller scale. On a grander stage, the Big Night event for retail customers now stretches over two nights. In 2002, the first Big Night featured Blue Band, the originator of the event, and the second presented Unox and Knorr. In all, sixty thousand retailers attended.

In short, the show goes on. And so does the power of growth. "Once people have felt the freedom and they begin to lead, you can never take that feeling away," said Gunning as he watched from afar what was happening in VdBN. In 2001 and again in 2002, stretch targets were achieved. The Foods business registered double-digit growth. The Fats business, with Janti and Conny in charge, increased volumes in 2001 and then in 2002 achieved the "impossible"—their business had top-line growth of 10 percent.

An Enterprise Culture in Unilever

Unilever began to hear its own wake-up call when its stock price declined 14 percent in 1999 and failed to recover in 2000. The ability of the company to grow was being called into question. Various frameworks for growth, issued from the corporate center, didn't turn things around. At a meeting of top leaders, one attendee called the question: Unilever had to move "beyond intellectual discussions and take action."

In January 2001, the two chairmen of Unilever, Antony Burgmans and Niall FitzGerald started their own "path to growth" and took their top hundred leaders to a four-day outbreak in Costa Rica. As described by one participant, "the jackets came off and the jungle shirts went on."[2] Supported by professional facilitators, they shared their emotional lifelines, talked about their personal and collective vision, and discussed the current realities of their business units. They also rode in Jeeps, traveled in boats, hiked in rainforests, and slept alongside one another in tents.

Tex Gunning participated in the program as one of Unilever's top leaders, as did Anthonie Stal. "There never was a conscious decision to go and study what was done at VdBN," explained Arjan Overwater, the VP of HR assisting in Unilever's transformation. "We were on our own path to discovery. No question though that VdBN served as an inspiration and aspiration."[3]

Indeed, over the next months, many of the familiar messages about growing people and the business became part of the new vocabulary in Unilever. Said the chairmen in a pamphlet outlining an emerging "enterprise culture" in the Unilever:

> Growing a business is only possible if we grow ourselves. For this we need leadership vision and inspiration. As leaders we have to feel emotionally connected with our business agenda and continuously build our own leadership.

"A collective feeling arose that the business was not separate from us and that we should get more personally involved," remarked one of the Costa Rica participants. These feelings were echoed in subsequent workshops run by country chairmen, business group presidents, and other executives. Over the next year some twenty "enterprise for growth workshops" built leadership teams throughout Unilever.

Unilever's two chairmen also led journeys with the next generation of leaders—160 of them—to Iceland and Croatia. "These journeys provided an extraordinary setting and a unique context to connect with a group of young leaders and together with them shape the long-term vision of the company," explained Overwater. One of the future leaders remarked: "The outcome was a deep realization that 'they' do not exist, it's all about what I want to achieve and what I can do about it."

As of this writing the reshaping of Unilever into an enterprise culture is very much in motion. The top hundred leaders continue to meet annually and workshops cascade down the company. And ever-new ways to develop and grow emerge. For example, Tex and Arjan recently cohosted a gathering joining Unilever managers with select change agents and figures from psychology, biology, arts, and religion to "widen the horizon" and augment thinking about transformation and growth.

With a focus on four hundred leading brands, Unilever has made some gains on its path to growth.[4] In 2001, for instance, food sales increased 4.1 percent—a rate neatly matched in the recession year 2002. This is a significant improvement over prior years and, according to company reports, leaves it on target to achieve 6–7 percent growth objectives per annum. Profitability continues to climb, but not the stock price, as yet.

Where is Unilever's brightest growth opportunity? Asia.

Back to Asia

Returning to Asia, Gunning carried with him his beliefs about the necessity of growth and experiences building a business through people. But on each of these counts, he would have to stretch his thinking and experiment with a broader transformational agenda.

When Gunning arrived in Singapore in 2000, the financial crisis of the late 1990s in Asia was abating and Unilever's Asian business overall was growing organically by double digits. The challenge was to refocus strategies from surviving a crisis to achieving sustainable growth.

On one hand, Unilever Asia would need to dramatically upgrade its management talent and systems to sustain profitable growth. On the other hand, sustained growth would also depend on bringing the middle class and especially the poor into economic development in Asia, and very much on improving the quality of life for Asian consumers.

Waking Up to Sustainability

In January 2001, some 150 Asian leaders embarked on an outbreak to Malaysia, where together they experienced the beginnings of a wake-up call about sustainability. Their planes from Kuala Lumpur landed in Sarawak, on the island of Borneo, and they boarded buses to a local beach strewn with refuse. There an Asian expert reviewed with them the devastation of Asia's natural environment and its links to industrial and economic development. In small groups, as they carted around trash bags and cleaned up the beach, they talked about the significance and implications of what they had heard and were experiencing first hand. Later that evening, back in their hotel ballroom, they intermingled at tables piled with newspaper articles and laptops keyed to Internet resources covering the Asian economy, consumer aspirations, demographics, environment, lifestyles, East versus West, and other sustainability issues. Their task was to prepare a newspaper, *Vision 2010*, designed to stimulate thinking about Asia's future—and their own.

Over the next two days the leaders shared their lifelines, talked of their personal aspirations and worries, and visited with an indigenous tribe of Panan people. A long, physically demanding and heart-wrenching hike through the Panans' increasingly deforested lands led to earnest discussion of the cultural and environmental costs of economic growth in Asia. This moving connection to an ancient people and a splendid natural environment spoiled by "progress" made its way into Unilever's vision in Asia.

"This was a perfect setting to start creating Vision 2010 for Asia," explained one of the participants. "We were able to move from discovering self to building a mental picture about the future with a clear direction of where to go and where to be. To be in the jungles of Borneo helped us to feel and see the potential in this region—to almost feel and touch the vision."

"The beauty of nature and majesty of the place helped deepen our insights about our roles as leaders and individuals on this earth," said another. "We began the event by talking about the global impact of industries on the environment. We experienced that individuals can make a difference, and together we are very powerful."

Everyone recognized that this outbreak was but one step toward Unilever Asia's transformation. There were even more complex issues to be dealt with, and fishbowl discussions in Borneo began to tackle them one by one: the participation of women on Asian management boards, the relative number of Asian board members versus European expats, and more. These messages and vision 2010 were not just shared among top leaders of the Asia region; a group of "young leaders" were invited to join this outbreak and to meet regularly thereafter.

Raising Voices to Be Heard

The first Asian Young Leaders' Forum (YLF) met in Singapore, shortly after Gunning's appointment as president of the business.[5] Country chairmen selected up to three young candidates for the forum that was aimed at developing a new generation of Asian leaders for Unilever and would operate as a peer network and support group.

The invitation to the YLF caught many of the young leaders by surprise:

> When I was sent to the group, I was not sure why. "Who is this president?" I asked myself. "What does he want?" During our first meeting, it was clear to me that the objective was to build leaders. We were challenged to triple the growth for the business, seemingly impossible at the time. We were there to become leaders so that we can do the impossible. The question I had in my mind then was: "How real is this? How committed is he?"

Gunning took on the development of some thirty young leaders—from finance, production, marketing, and human resources—as his personal mission. Following the Sarawak retreat, the young leaders spent a week together for *Seven Habits* training. Since then, there have been YLF meetings twice a year. In 2001, the young leaders met in Danang, Vietnam, in April and again that November. After completing their business and personal development agenda for the spring meeting, they left their comfortable South China Sea resort to visit the markets and homes of an impoverished hamlet nearby. There they also met Van Tan Hoc, founder of the

Village of Hope, an orphanage home to 180 displaced and disabled children, to learn firsthand what it takes to bring a "big dream" to life with little but "an abundance of hope."

In Bangalore, India, in May 2002, the YLF again took up the question of sustainability—this time directly. Teams of the young leaders went to Delhi, Mumbai, and Bangalore to visit local markets, talk to consumers, meet with retailers, and look at the many lifestyles in India. Then they convened to prepare a business plan for introducing ice tea into India. Their challenge was not only to launch a profitable product but also to develop a pricing structure and distribution plan to get it into the hands of India's poorer population—the 600 million villagers who reside at the bottom of the economic pyramid. They presented their proposal to Vindi Banga, chairman of Hindustan Lever, the Indian operating company, and had it critiqued by C. K. Prahalad—who together with Hindustan Lever has introduced important new ideas on shrinking the gap between the rich and poor.[6]

The company's transformational agenda and legacy depends on creating a cadre of Asian executives who can lead sustainable growth. The young leaders in this forum felt empowered when they were invited to join the top Asian business leaders in creating Vision 2010. "It was a turning point when we faced the management board and declared that we would be leading this revolution," recalled one of the young leaders. "We were elevated as a voice to be heard. We were invited to lead the company's next phase of growth," explained another. "We began to feel that we can really do something."

Forming a Humane Business Community

The feeling among the young Asian leaders that they could really do something about the business tells just one part of the story. "We started the forum knowing that it was about business, but somewhere along the way, we forgot about that and instead learned about humanity!" exclaimed one of the young leaders after his visit to the orphanage in Danang. "It's all about realizing that you want to touch other people's lives. When you connect with others here and share amazing experiences and you face humanity, you become a better person. That remains with you."

Why is being confronted with your own humanity such a profound, moving experience? And why do we need a reminder to feel our own humanity? If connecting with others is so human, so innate, why do we lose this capability in organizational life? These were the questions the young leaders were confronted with at the May 2002 YLF meeting. As Gunning explained it:

> When faced with our own humanity, we become aware of all the love and pain we carry. We reconnect to our souls, and we meet again our true selves. When we see authenticity or meet indigenous peoples, when we connect with nature, observe animals, play with children, and talk to the elderly, we can have such experiences. But how do you make such experiences meaningful? How do you capture those feelings and move on to a higher level of consciousness and make it part of your life?

The answers lay partly in reflection, both in the inward look for meaning and values, strengths and limitations, doubts and hopes, and in outwardly expressing them to others:

> Reflection is one of the most powerful tools for learning and for growth. In the humane organization, because it is safe, people may share feelings and thoughts, or may test their intuitions freely. Reflection, both individually and collectively, finds a fertile environment if people truly live in community.

Gunning's reflections at the end of the gathering spoke to the importance of creating a business environment that appeals to innate human needs and actively promotes a true sense of community. Still, acknowledging the complexities of growth and sustainability in Asia and the foibles of humankind and his own leadership, he closed his message to this group of emerging young leaders on a cautionary note:

As leaders we can have major impact. We always talk about the positive side of leading. This gives people meaning, and builds communities of support. But then there is the other side of the coin. You can also have a huge negative impact. If you get it wrong, you frustrate people and create a nongenerative environment where there is pain and serious consequences. Some decisions have far more profound effects than one thinks about. You may sometimes have to act against the company culture. We have to make sure there are people around us who can see and correct our mistakes. And we have to have the humbleness to listen to them and act on it.

Part VI

Takeaways for Leading Change

Chapter 14

Change Models and Methods

> We achieved transformation by looking in the
> mirror and seeing that our world wasn't the world
> we should be in. New leaders showed us that it was
> like Plato's cave—we needed to come out in the
> sun and see: What is right and what is wrong?
> What do we have to change and how?
>
> —*Brand director*

As researchers and practitioners, we sought to identify the pattern of actions that stimulated and directed VdBN's transformation. A starting point is to look at the ideas, models, and methods introduced by new leaders and embraced by the company in everyday practice. What stimulated the transformation of this Unilever business was the necessity to grow. "Growth is a big issue—much bigger than it has ever been. Growth means winning. Growth means wealth. In the new economy," Gunning went on, "growth has become a necessity."

This message took hold readily among the more business-minded managers and staff, who could see its implications for profitability, career development, and job challenge. Said a finance manager, "If your top line is not growing, your bottom line will sooner or later collapse. That's simple mathematics. Plus, if you don't grow, there is no goal for people to work for, no good opportunities for promotion, and you're managing something totally unexciting." Others had to experience the meaning of growth in their jobs and come to terms with it personally. "During the process of

the last few years, I became aware that our people are not our ene-
mies. In fact, they are the most powerful force we have," reflected a
marketing manager. "This made me realize that we should be
judged by more than our financial results. We should also be judged
by the legacy of personal growth that we leave behind. This made
a big change in how I see my role and in what I expect from the
people who work with me."

The Pyramid of Growth

Grow people and grow the business. These are the favored aims behind many business transformations in the United States, Europe,
and Asia. Easy to say them, but what does it take to bring them into
being? In this case, leading the company from a turnaround to
transformation, from a vision of doubling volumes to creating a
legacy of growth, would mean developing an organization capable
of growing year after year. But most of the current leaders and staff
had developed their mindsets and skills in declining or at best low-
growth markets. Thus the script for leading change here called not
only for reinventing strategy but also for devising new structures
and developing new capabilities at every level in the company.

Peter Drucker contends that companies' rise and fall can be
traced to the validity of management's "theory of the business."[1]
This theory has to do with management's assumptions about the
marketplace, understandings of their business, how often and how
honestly they test their views, and their capacities to make needed
change. In the first learning conference at UVGN, Gunning presented his own management theory in the form of a pyramid (Figure 14.1). This theory evolved through experience and was tested
and elaborated over the course of the next five years by the chairman, management board, and business unit and team leaders. It
guided the changes in strategy and product innovation, and in organization structure and people management, that transformed the
business to double-digit growth.

Figure 14.1 Pyramid of Growth

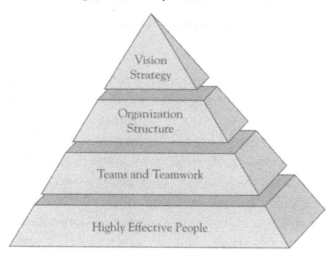

Vision and Strategy

At the peak of the pyramid is business vision—along with the strategies, tactics, and programs needed to bring it to life. Beginning with the UVGN transformation in 1995, emphasis was given to volume growth (2X Growth) and to "step-change" improvements in innovation, quality, and cost. The VdBN merger in 1997 added more brands to the Foods portfolio. Attention turned, accordingly, to segmenting customers, prioritizing initiatives, gaining market share, finding new channels, and opening up new business categories.

Within the business units, there were strategic reviews and new initiatives:

- In-depth analyses of the market, consumer trends, and product portfolios
- Redefinition of competitors and competitive space (for example, candy, coffee, tea)
- Benchmarking of best practices (for example, Heineken, Coca-Cola)

- Innovation with new products and rebranding of existing ones
- Aggressive moves to counter competition and grocer house brands

On the Foods side, for example, strategy reviews revealed opportunities in the out-of-home market and among consumers on the go. Taking action on these opportunities meant reconnecting with food consumers, seeing the business from the outside in, and repositioning soup as a snack. The result was the launch of Cup-a-Office, new "John the Manager" commercials, and a nearly 60 percent sales increase in the first year.

These strategic moves were energized and informed by vision. "Yes, of course, it was partly market research. And it was partly the experience of salespeople," said a young marketer on the Cup-a-Soup team. "But it came down to this: 'What is our common dream? What do we want to achieve?' Everyone had this dream that it would be great if people used our product every day."

New strategy and vision were crucial in Fats, too. The project leader of the Bertolli brand sandwich team noted, "The breakthrough in growth was achieved because we worked from a good consumer-oriented strategy. A clear vision of the category and brand unlocked enthusiasm and created positive energy."

Organization Structure

The reorganizations in both UVGN and VdBN were a second level of change demanded by the pyramid of growth. Closing plants, selling assets, and laying off staff came as a shock. But what made it all palatable, and even attractive, to remaining employees was that they saw very real benefits. "Fairly early on we saw results," said a marketing manager. "It was done in an unconventional way, but people were not really unhappy. If you want to make an omelet, you have to break eggs."

More difficult to accept, at least for some in management, was the delayering of their management ranks and the disempowerment of some established, long-time executives as young leaders took over their responsibilities and jobs. The changes created a meritocratic work environment, unleashing energy and creativity to drive the business forward. "We had given workers responsibility, we had motivated them, but only when we took a few layers out did people assume real responsibility," recalled a finance director, who elaborated, "What really changed is the authority level—'who do you need to talk to for approval?' Not everything had to be referred back to the board or to the head of the unit. Individuals or smaller teams could take initiatives and just do it."

New organizational structures created over the five years included

- Work units organized and aligned with manufacturing and marketing-sales responsibilities
- Business units divided into value creation (innovation and brand development) and value delivery (category and account management) functions
- Select product groups run as stand-alone businesses
- Factory lines run with profit-and-loss accountability
- Work teams formed and team leaders charged with running the business

These organizational changes won approval and acceptance at every level. The decision to go with 180 team leaders based on the respect they commanded rather than the position in the hierarchy that they occupied was a breakthrough. "Leaders throughout the organization now actually run the business," said one observer. "To achieve a transformation, you had to get them involved." The character and culture of the company evolved to a cooperative, collaborative, community-minded organization. "In the beginning we were all individuals and we were fighting each other," said a factory team leader. "Now there is working together instead of working against one another."

Teams and Teamwork

Growing the business via teams had two distinct elements. The first was teams formed in the factories that used the Total Preventive Maintenance (TPM) process improvement methodology. Developed in Japan, and used throughout Unilever, TPM reduced maintenance costs and improved factory efficiencies. Several team leaders and operators went to Japan to learn the methodology and three of the VdBN factories earned coveted TPM rewards.

Later, after the 180-leader group was formed, there were annual team leader retreats and periodic training sessions featuring a mix of Covey and community-building concepts, exercises on teaming and group reflection, and often an outdoor adventure such as biking, hiking, and the like. Many work teams held circle discussions to talk about their progress, deal with team issues, and share more of their personal lives and aspirations. They also staged their own events to build team spirit, going out together to enjoy each other's company and develop connections that went beyond the job at hand.

The impact of teaming rippled from the team leaders down to factory operators and up to their bosses. Some reflections:

- *From a factory operator:* My feeling was OK, I did not know what was going to happen, but I had trust. We had to change together. We started working in teams in 1997. And many things changed. All sorts of new tasks and responsibilities were pushed down to the workers. The culture changed too.

- *From a factory team leader:* We made agreements about how the team would function best. About how we would compose the team and what one would expect from the people. That was a piece of openness and honesty. We also talked about what would be the best ingredients for a team and how we would manage them. What was an obstacle, for instance, was that people talked about each other, but not directly to the person concerned. Now when something goes wrong, you tell the person involved, and not just talk about their mistakes behind their back.

- *From a factory director*: A key breakthrough for me was the realization that I could optimize business results by facilitating the work of people rather than trying to do it all myself. Basically, giving trust rather than orders. This happened in a rather hopeless situation. I just focused on establishing a sense of urgency and setting direction. My people did the work with far better results than I could have dreamed of. We increased plant output 300 percent.

Highly Effective People

At the base of the pyramid is the hard work and development of the people in the organization. Over the course of the five years, for instance, more than a thousand people in VdBN went through training based on Stephen Covey's *Seven Habits of Highly Effective People*. A number of managers were certified as Covey trainers and key concepts in the program became part of everyday language in the company. The personal insights were far-reaching as well:

- *From a marketing manager*: A major breakthrough for me was during a Covey course where deep down inside I felt I was OK. A very silly insight, written down on a yellow sheet. . . . A very emotional insight when lived through that moment. . . . It was the start of a new period in my life when I felt myself less and less dependent on the judgments of others.
- *From a factory operator*: Personally the biggest insight from Covey was learning to live proactively. I became much more aware of my actions and reactions. I began to understand our management philosophy much better. For me being proactive has to do with vision and creating your future.
- *From a sales manager*: I try to listen to others, and also try to respect the opinions of others. How did I learn to do this?

  By holding up the mirror to my own face once in a while.

  By admitting that you cannot do it all.

By conversations at home and reflections, asking "What have I learned?"

Through continuous experimentation—at levels of vision and strategy, structure and systems, through to teaming and personal development—management's pyramid of growth was tested and refined. One HR manager internalized it in this way: "You know the pyramid of growth. It is the basis of everything. Personal growth leads to business growth and business growth leads to personal growth." What is missing in the pyramid, however, is a dynamic component—a way of knowing *when* to effect change and *how*. Here, again, a theory of change would deepen over three transformation cycles.

Transformation Cycles

The transformation in VdBN was punctuated by several action cycles—each with its own themes and characteristics (see Figure 14.2). The UVGN turnaround commenced with a dramatic call to action to "prevent the ship from sinking." Then people were mobilized to grow volume and regain market share, a phase labeled "building the business."

The cycle repeated in the VdBN merger, starting with the call to action of "a new beginning." The business mobilized around the theme of "competing for the future" with attention going to building community (inside the company) and connecting with retailers and consumers (outside the firm).

Figure 14.2 Cycles of Transformation

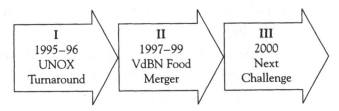

| I
1995–96
UNOX
Turnaround | II
1997–99
VdBN Food
Merger | III
2000
Next
Challenge |

The team leaders' event in early 2000 marked the start of a third transformation cycle. The call to action was to face the challenges of the New Economy. As events played out, this would be carried forward at VdBN under new leadership.

There are many dynamics in transformation cycles.[2] Psychologist Kurt Lewin, for instance, uses unfreezing-movement-refreezing to represent stages of change in the physical and psychological states of living things—from organisms to social systems. William Bridges surveys these phases as expressed in literature and in life and speaks of endings, transitions, and new beginnings. And anthropologists, documenting the sweep of change in cultures and societies, see periods of upheaval, followed by conflict and reordering, and finally reintegration.

Over the past several decades, business and the social sciences have also defined processes for initiating and managing organizational change, for example:

- *Wake-Up Call:* Awakening people to the need for change
- *Current Reality:* Analyzing the current situation and possible options
- *Vision for Future:* Defining aspirations and a dream for the future
- *Mobilizing Support:* Enlisting followers and dealing with resistance
- *Implementing Change:* Changing hard and soft aspects of the business

Each is well known in generic form to business leaders and change agents. And they were all a part of the process of change here. For instance, it is incontrovertible that both UVGN and VdBN needed to be awakened to the need for change. "In 1995, we were still very much behind, we hardly spoke about competition. It was cost management rather than opportunity management," recalled a UVGN commercial director. "I can't say I was very excited back then." That situation was not any better at VdBN in 1997. "VdBN was not ready for the new century," said a brand manager. "We were old-fashioned in our methods, produced our products in our old ways, and were an outdated company."

The arrival of new leadership at UVGN sped up change. "Every signal in their first months indicated that we would change every element of the business, whether it was competition, industry, market attractiveness, brands, or how we operated together with the trade," a marketing manager recalled. "The business was turned upside down."

The changes at VdBN were equally dramatic. New ideas about food came from the "outside in." A new culture, in turn, was created from the "inside out." Said a sales service manager, "The biggest change came when the management board said we have to involve everybody in what we are trying to achieve. Board members made very clear that they also wanted to change, and they did. That set an example for the total business."

In each case, it took extensive communications to awaken people to current realities, break through denial, and create urgency for action. Attention-getting interventions, rich in substance and symbolism, and rigorous fact finding ensured that all employees understood the depth of problems and rallied behind a vision for change. Team leader outbreaks, work unit programs, and all-company learning conferences mobilized the entire organization. And implementation of the elements in the pyramid of growth aligned action and developed the capacity to transform at every level of the company.

Leading Change

The ambition to grow summoned a leader who could foresee new trends, translate ideas into action, engage, excite, and embolden an entire organization, and help people to embrace change as their friend. In realizing it, Gunning, according to people in VdBN, was by turns a tough bastard, a poet, a preacher, and an everyday mate. Like other successful leaders in business, he was guided by his own

The year of the merger   After the merger with UVGN, a top-to-bottom organizational review, and the revolution in the Foods group resulting in the ouster of its general manager, VdBN was in turmoil as 1997 drew to a close. A clip from the film *The Abyss* at the management conference in Antwerp in December hit the right nerve, pointing up the need for the company's leaders to connect intellectually and emotionally if they were to be a real team.

180 leaders in charge   The February 1998 "Ardennes Offensive" began the process of developing 180 VdBN leaders into a team committed to the objective of growth. In the ruins of a medieval monastery in Belgium's Ardennes forest, they plotted and shared their emotional lifelines as a first step toward building trust and respect for one another and bringing emotions into the business.

Commitment to grow together   After a rocky start, the February 1999 "leadership journey" to Scotland culminated in an exhausting but exhilarating climb to the summit of the Corrain on the Isle of Skye. The experience produced new notions and conversations about how the company's leaders could help and support one another in pursuing the "legacy of growth."

Making commitment visible Tex Gunning at the table in the kitchen installed in his office space, where VdBN leaders would prepare lunch as part of their regular business meetings to symbolize their commitment to growing the foods business. As they cooked and ate together, their relationships deepened as did their appreciation of the way the market experienced their products and their competition.

Company-wide growth and community   From their inception in 1996 at
UVGN, annual learning conferences brought together all company employees
for a day of learning and fun in ever more elaborate and challenging events.
Up to 1800 people at a time, in settings ranging from theme parks to exhibition halls to football arenas, would learn about the state of the company, work
together in discussions and exercises led by their team leaders, and celebrate
their successes with a huge party at the end of the day. Sophisticated live
video, dozens of giant TV monitors, high-quality sound systems, live entertainment, take-away gifts, good food, and fun exercises made these events a powerful way to involve all employees in the ongoing transformation.

Wake-up call III   By February 2000 VdBN had transformed itself from a no-growth business to one that had achieved remarkable results and growth in many areas. Now the question was how to accelerate that growth. On their last outbreak under Gunning's leadership, VdBN's 180 team leaders traveled to the Wadi Rum desert of Jordan to hear the next challenge: "If we want to grow Unilever, we have to re-invent ourselves."

Learning from the past   To prepare for "the next level of inspiration and aspiration," VdBN leaders created timelines of key events for themselves and their businesses over the past five years. They traveled by plane, Jeep, and camel to Jerusalem, the Dead Sea, and Wadi Rum, where they explored their history together, highlighted lessons learned, and made plans for their future, as individuals and company leaders. Many here would say their breakthroughs had been not only intellectual and emotional, but also spiritual.

Passing the torch   The final scene in VdBN's trip to the desert is played out inside Ed Deir, an ancient Nabatean monastery built into the cliffs of Petra, Jordan. After three days of reflecting on their five years working together, celebrating the growth of their business, and setting their sights on new challenges, the "tribe" bids goodbye to Gunning, who passes his torch to the incoming chairman and challenges the company's leaders to continue the legacy of growth.

theories about business, growth, and change. And, over the five years in the Netherlands, he put those theories into practice, continued to experiment and learn, and ultimately led the business to double-digit growth.

Said one team leader about the impact, "There were other change programs in the past. We had 'Total Quality Management,' we had 'Together Better,' and we had three other programs. We would say, 'Yeah, this is a good thing,' but we would go on with the daily work. With Tex, this was not possible. Every day he would remind you: 'Don't just go back to the daily work, you have to change, you have to grow.'"

To effect successful transformations on this scale required someone schooled in leading change.[3] Many commented on their leader's ability to wake up the organization, communicate a vision, mobilize support, deal with resistance, and make things happen. (See Exhibit 14.1.) Another important element was his storytelling—about business, products, and people matters, to be sure, and also about his own background, beliefs, aspirations, and failings. In time, board members, team leaders, and office and factory workers alike made these things a regular part of their own reflection, vocabulary, and conversation.

Of course, not everyone eagerly embraced these new practices or welcomed the transformational agenda. For instance, a revolutionary approach to change was a godsend for some. "Tex had a lot to offer in terms of how to transform the organization, the tools and staffing up the strategic review," said a marketing director. "I knew immediately this is what I had been looking for." But others found it overwhelming. "He was always throwing the group off its horse, never putting an end to things, never providing the stability for people to adapt to the changes. There was this constant question, 'Why does he keep throwing new challenges, keeping us in chaos all the time?'"

There were also critics of the chairman's vision and tactics. A buying director in the company remarked on the downside: "Tex has a lot of great ideas, but sometimes he is an unguided missile."

Exhibit 14.1 In Their Own Words:
Views on Transformational Leadership

Waking Up an Organization

"Leadership is about making choices. If you don't make choices you're just an administrator or a manager. And leadership is about having the vision of what the possibilities are and helping other people see those possibilities. Tex could come into hugely crashed situations, stand back, see what would need to be done and give people the choice. He created a structure in which people could see that they had a choice."

"We started to reorganize with some speed. There was discomfort all over the place. Our department changed directions three times over five years, which is a lot. People had to adapt to that. Priorities changed all the time. There was quite some movement but some initiatives failed completely."

Ideas and Vision

"What I really appreciate is the clarity. Tex seems to have some kind of antennae for developments in the market or with people. He has a visionary mind."

"By shifting the focus from the inside world to the outside world, suddenly the chairman assumed the role of the person who was inspiring the organization. Your reaction to him was 'do we have to go all the way?' This was a big change from the old days when you were the one who was the enthusiastic person and constantly felt people above you putting on the brakes and slowing you down."

Mobilizing Support

"In this business it is very difficult to change course for a new direction. If the people don't change, nothing will really happen. The biggest achievement of the management board was to make people aware that you have to act differently and have to change your approach to business."

"Tex was able to really get things into the mindset of the people from day one. By being there. Talking to people, really personal contact with people. Suddenly we had all kinds of groups meeting with each other. We mobilized ourselves."

Implementing Change

"He created the realization that there is dead wood and that you must cut it out of your organization rapidly. I was thrilled that there was a new leader who was able to really step up and change this business. On a personal level this is a leader from whom I can learn a lot."

"You can recognize Van den Bergh people in Holland by their language. They use a lot of management slang and business talk."

Said a senior HR official in Unilever, "There is a high level of admiration for his strategic capabilities, and thinking out of the box, but he needs to develop political sensitivity." Some also resented that he enlisted and depended on young leaders to transform UVGN and VdBN, labeling them his "clones."

The emotional high-and-lows of transformation and the intensity of the company events took a toll, too. "I'm convinced that you don't have to travel through deep valleys to be successful. I really believe you can gradually move upwards," said one of the old-time department managers. "My personal view is that you don't need drama to grow. I don't need to suffer before I can enjoy."

Wherever you stand on Gunning as a change leader, you will not be alone. Said an IT manager, "You knew what he was saying and his intentions behind what he did. He cared about growing this company, people's jobs, people's feelings and you could feel that. But some could not understand that. He was a real leader for many, but not for everyone."

Chapter 15

Change as Theater

You can provide the space for people to open up.
You direct, you follow the energy, and you feel
where the breakpoint is. But you never get exactly
what you want, because it's people.

—Eric Jan de Rooij, *organizer of outdoor events*

In the language of the arts and the discipline of performance studies, the events that brought changes to life at UVGN and VdBN can be termed *performances*.[1] In each instance, the actions of leaders and staff were more or less scripted, unfolding through a series of scenes. The events themselves were staged, with scrupulous attention to light, sound, and setting. There were costumes and props at hand, and the chairman cum director exerted a strong or light hand depending on the mood of the moment. Consider these examples of change as theater:

Scene 1: The Warehouse of Waste. A fleet of forklifts has amassed thousands of pallets, stacked floor to ceiling, full of food turned to waste. Some fourteen hundred employees tour the aisles and contemplate the massive loss. The stage is set for outbursts, then confrontation, and later for acknowledgment of problems and the first steps forward toward a new way.

Scene 2: Skating on Canals. Eighteen months later, skaters glide on frozen canals during *Elfstedentocht*, when waterways freeze over and the nation takes a day off for play. Alongside the frozen canals, some of those same fourteen hundred employees hand out bright orange hats that bear their company logo. Thousands of skaters appear on live national television and in newspapers wearing bright orange branded hats.

Scene 3: Soul-Searching in a Monastery. Another eighteen months on, in the cellar of a medieval monastery in Belgium's Ardennes forest, 180 team leaders hear their chairman speak from the heart about his upbringing, an abusive father, the highs and lows of his life. As he finishes, a young supervisor shouts out, "Thank you for sharing that. It's good to know you better." The leaders gathered then share their own life stories with one another.

Scene 4: Passing the Torch at Petra. Two years more, the chairman, his voice muffled by tears, announces, "We have done it, transformed ourselves and our business. That's it, I am gone." The chairman's successor embraces him and a band of young leaders pledge to keep the spirit alive. The assembled mass winds its way out of the torchlit temple and into a long night of feasting, dance, and song.

The Warehouse Scene

Let's look again at the awakening in the warehouse in theatrical terms. The staging is dramatic:

- An early morning bus ride to an unknown destination
- Secrecy about the trip's intent and the part they are about to play
- Stacked pallets whose meaning emerges as the tour progresses
- Signs detailing the contents, costs, and causes of the mess
- Company officials costumed in white lab coats to amplify the effect

As performance, the tour of the warehouse of waste immerses employees in an unfamiliar and unexpected reality. The sights before them shock, the smells nauseate, and the sound effects, added to the video made for those who could not attend, superimpose another layer of showmanship: Mozart's Requiem piped over loud-speakers. This act ends with an aptly staged scene: forklifts move the pallets from the warehouse to a nearby pit where the waste is buried.

The idea that change follows a script should not surprise. Indeed, Noel Tichy's well-known framework for organizational change characterizes it as a "three act drama."[2] In most such uses, however, drama is used as a *metaphor* for managerial activity. By comparison, in this case, the drama was an individual and collective *experience*. Indeed, we would contend that participating in the performance was itself transformative. Gunning and his team took on new roles—and through them new personae—as they performed; and their work took on new meaning and significance. Their warehouse theatrics, the first act of their drama, was a harbinger of further transformation of themselves and their business.

The Skating Scene

The skating performance is a different kind of theater in which the performance is largely unscripted and the audience drives the show. Much of it was improvised:

- The orange hats were purchased with no plans for how to use them.
- The idea to link them to outdoor ice-skating was a last-minute leap of imagination.
- The performance was wholly dependent on cooperative weather (freeze-overs do not happen every year).
- The staff had only the loosest direction on where to gather and how to get their countrymen in costume.
- The fourteen hours of live television and then print media coverage, a boost to the brand and the people, was a surprise.

It's likely that few of the skaters who were by turns audience members and actors appreciated in the moment how their costuming, vigor, and color choreography made revival of the brand part of the spectacle. Later, the staff's dash into the frigid North Sea waters, imagined only as a cast party, turned into yet another performance.

There is some symmetry between the warehouse and the skating scenes: the symbolic death of the old culture in the burial pit and the subsequent rebirth of a new culture through baptism in the sea. But consider two other aspects of the skating performance. First, it was a one-time event. Coupled with the widespread media coverage, its uniqueness made the experience even more memorable. Second, the performance was successful in part because people had a chance to *play*. In a mix of improvisation and street theater, the staff had fun chasing after skaters, surprising them with hats, getting them into the act, and then watching the swathe of orange hats glide against white snow. The instinctually appealing aspects of play and interplay, with laughter and hilarity, made this a transformative experience for employees and consumers alike.

In Scenes Beyond . . .

The first team leader meeting in the Ardennes moved further into what anthropologists term *deep play*, wherein fundamental ideas and cultural codes are open to inspection.[3] In this sense, the Ardennes and the subsequent company-wide learning conferences enabled people to play with their identities and culture. In reflective conversations—very much part of the performance—they talked about themselves, their work, and the difficulties of truly connecting as people. They in turn made a commitment to be authentic, to listen deeply, and to treat one another with respect. As one attendee summed up the meaning: "For me it represented a major turnaround . . . the way leaders and then all the people of Van den Bergh showed something personal about themselves. The example showed that I am more than just a 'working' person in the company. The 'whole' person is welcomed."

Expressed in cultural terms, the team leaders' events and learning conferences gave the company a heart. By the time of the journey to the desert, does it go too far to say that the company—and its people—had developed a soul?

Process Versus Performance

The idea that leadership, management, customer service, indeed almost any kind of work can be understood as a performing art has intellectual merit for scholars and decided appeal to many practitioners. There are several comparison points between the elements of, say, organizational and theatrical performance. Consider some of the *process versus performance* distinctions we saw as the VdBN story unfolded (Exhibit 15.1).

Plan Versus Script

Processes are based on plans. Mission statements, the goals that they express, and the activities needed to reach them lay out what has to be done and the steps involved. Although the elements differ in, say, strategic, financial, and operational plans, what they specify in toto is *what* has to happen to get the job done right.

Scripts serve this function in performances. But the script goes deeper and further by elaborating and detailing *how* things should be done. One could quibble about this distinction by referencing tactical plans, instructions, and other ways by which plans are elaborated, activities specified, and controls designed. Instead, see it as

Exhibit 15.1 Process Versus Performance

Process	Performance
Plan	Script
Steps	Scenes
Staff	Cast
Do	Act
Manager	Director
Deliver	Delight

a matter of shading and intention. Consider, for example, the high compliments we apply to plans: a good plan is logical, sensible, sound. While a script conveys a plan, it also speaks to the expression of emotion, suggests how to bring activity to life, and reminds that *art* is to be performed. That's what makes a good script beautiful.

Dramatization, in turn, brings a script to life. The gathering of 180 team leaders in the Ardennes, for example, was carefully scripted to acknowledge the upheaval in VdBN, give voice to emotions, introduce new ways of doing business, and ultimately reconnect people.[4] Recall that the merger of UVGN and VdBN produced a culture clash between the "farmers" and the "university types" and then revolution and chaos. In the aftermath, the business was pulled together but its people were disconnected. Look at elements of the dramaturgy in the Ardennes to see how this was brought to life:

- The exercise with people playing the part of cynics or believers narrates tensions and doubts in the company, along with aspirations and hopes.

- The sharing of lifelines asks people to speak personally, opens up emotions, and affirms a common humanity.

- The famous fishbowl reveals different outlooks on the business, demonstrates top leaders' vulnerability, and establishes new terms of engagement for dealing with difficult issues.

- The construction of a circular, wood-framed, cloth-covered village—where all have to work, talk, and sleep together—creates a bond that says "we are all in this together."

These activities were scripted to engage people individually and collectively, and had physical and symbolic, as well as intellectual and emotional, components. But the script also created the space *and* gave people the space to reconnect—the overall aim of the performance. The revelations and heartfelt reactions—the unscripted human drama—were authentic and of-the-moment, and the bonds formed were based on deep empathy and genuine feeling.

By comparison, there was no elaborate script for the "passing of the torch" in Petra. Rites of passage like this are universal: tribes everywhere, ancient and modern, use them to mark time and achievements. But there is no question that it was dramatically staged. Many hours went into the design of this experience to create the right setting and mood to produce hoped-for results. All the participants—team leaders in the business, along with executives, various facilitators, and a support team—together created the performance. They played their self-defined parts very well and the actions unfolded in a manner that was moving and right.

Steps Versus Scenes

In comparing process steps to performance scenes, we find a similar emphasis on *what* instead of *how*. Both dictate sequence, flow, and timing. Attention to the scene also stresses the emotive aspects of action and aims at the experience of being there. In this light, one could argue that precisely because the warehouse awakening was arranged as scenes, it had such a powerful impact. Compare these reactions to the informative and performative features of the warehouse event:

> *Informative:* "At the warehouse we were told what we were doing was not right. We got more information. We got to see the numbers. There were quality problems. That was a shock for me because people did their best and they were never told. This factory is our bread. If it goes bad with the factory, it goes bad with us."

> *Performative:* "The whole thing was definitely masterminded. The structure of the event was to introduce the strategic situation . . . in a very graphic and powerful way. Exultant music. Piles of products. The stamp "reject." "Oh God! This is a warehouse full of reject product!"

This reminds of the importance of timing and scenery. The team leaders' 1999 demanding hike up the craggy, mountainous

Corrain on the Isle of Skye in Scotland, for example, provided an uplifting close to an otherwise flat and soggy two-day experience. The desert of Wadi Rum is one of those majestic places where you feel immediately in harmony with the universe. Your frame of reference shifts: There is something much bigger than you are and you feel a part of it. Engaging in dialogue and addressing business issues in such a place opens up new possibilities. VdBN team leaders could reflect with their minds and their hearts; and their reflections were both thoughtful and soulful.

Staff Versus Cast

Work and acting join in the roles people assume on the job and on stage. Indeed, the organizational use of the term borrows from theater precisely to communicate work's performance dimensions. Still, people attach a different meaning to being members of a cast rather than members of a staff. Cast members are expected to become their characters through imaging, rehearsing, costuming, and makeup. This asks more of people than, say, most job descriptions and demands more presence than just showing up.

Being in a cast involves teamwork and, as with any high-performing team, everyone has to play their part for the show to succeed. But theatrical performers are so integral to the performance that everyone gets listed in the credits—still a rarity for many teams. Being part of a theatrical troupe is also distinctive; show business has undeniable cachet. Recognizing this, top entertainment, dining, and transportation companies (Disney, Hard Rock Café, and Southwest Airlines among them) have dramatized their customer service and stage it every day.

The value of being part of the show extends backstage and even into the audience. The production crew at VdBN, some of whom had other "day jobs" in the company, for example, increased in its size and aspirations even as the events increased in their scale and artistry. The outdoor event organizers and group facilitators integrated their separate expertise and adapted that to the themes—

competing, teaming, clanning—of the transformation. Employees would alternate as audience and actors at the all-company learning conferences, whether sharing life stories, working on team exercises, singing songs, or reflecting on camera about what they learned. And, at the Big Night events, grocers throughout Holland, from store-owners to shelf-stockers to cashiers, took their turns as customers of VdBN and contributors to its transformative events.

Do Versus Act

While doing and acting seem synonymous, acting as performance art has some distinguishing features. The creation of an alternative reality through play frees imagination, generates energy, and opens possibilities for new directions. In turn, precisely because actors are playing, and the experience is make-believe, they can reflect from a distance and, in so doing, learn something about their art and themselves. Certainly the use of role-play in management training is based on these assumptions.

Acting out new behavior can have an impact on individuals and companies that extends beyond any particular performance. Events at VdBN encouraged people to follow a path of personal growth and helped to align individual and business goals. Sharing their deepest fears and aspirations—in business and in personal life—built a strong basis for trust and community. And working on vision in this context created an inevitable connection between personal breakthroughs and breakthroughs in the business.

- *From an HR manager:* For a couple of days you're in a completely different surrounding. Flying in an airplane, biking, canoeing, and walking is something you don't do every day. You're more or less lost, so all the experiences have an impact on you as a person and on your work with your colleagues.

- *From an IT manager:* Today I would describe the company culture as playful. Playful, loose, creative, always changing directions. Playing is good; you are open to new possibilities.

Manager Versus Director

We do not need to repeat the countless tracts telling managers to orchestrate, choreograph, coach, and in other ways add to the artistry of organizational performance.[5] But it is worth reminding that managers cum directors benefit from artistic sensibilities and skills.[6] They have the authority and responsibility to ensure the integrity of a performance—its narrative, presentation, and flow. "When you do these events," says Eric Jan de Rooij, organizer of outdoor events, "you go into them with a certain mindset of what you want to get out. An event is like a magnifying glass. You can really see where your company is. And people can see each other. With such transparency you can easily define next steps. But strong leadership is the key to the success of the event, and to what happens afterwards."

It also helps to have an eye for symbolism and ear for when things go flat. Hear Gunning on his own practice:

> There you need this emergent thing. Continuous feeling and sensing and changing plans accordingly. Keeping in touch with what is happening moment by moment. Because that is when miracles happen. And you see that everything is interrelated, and needs to follow a particular sequence. And if one misses out on one tiny little opportunity it may all fall apart.

Deliver Versus Delight

This distinction between the sought after end of process versus performance is admittedly arbitrary. Nevertheless, there is a tendency in process management to focus so much on concrete, measurable deliverables that creativity and fun are simply driven out of the process. Indeed, in service of efficiency and with an eye to gaining control, processes become compartmentalized, routinized, and lifeless. In many instances, processes are equated to bureaucracy; to put an idea into a process is tantamount to slowly killing it.

Performances, by comparison, aim to delight in their delivery, reinforce the aesthetic agenda, and remind us of the life-giving power of art. Of course, many mass-produced performances—and even creatively fashioned ones—prove mediocre or miss their mark. The ones that we have looked at here have tried to embody and carry forward aspirations for change. These deliverables and their delivery necessarily include the intangibles that Gunning spoke of and artistry in the overall production.

In performance studies, the "social drama" of life and the "aesthetic drama" of performance are depicted in a figure eight with each either contributing to or detracting from the other. At VdBN, work-life concerns and performance effects were tightly married, so that each enriched the other. As a Dutch staffer cum cast member said of the company's learning conferences, these were not just events in themselves:

> With no continuity, with no team building, we would not have results. We are one small company in Delft and I see every year we are working with two thousand people. We talked about ourselves in business, about the power we had in our own hands. People spoke about their own practice, not from the book, but from their experience. For me that is gold.

Performing and Learning

Marking progress and creating change in organizations via events is still a new idea. Despite budding interest in performativity among managers and scholars and the exciting potential of the "experience economy," there is not much received wisdom on how to stage performances that are truly meaningful in companies.[7] The performances described here shared some of the following design characteristics:

- Leadership performed actively and visibly with staff. Some of this had to do with legitimizing theatrics and some with role modeling and setting a tone.

- Experiences were scripted and staged at individual, group, and collective levels. The rationale here is to build capacity from the bottom up and stimulate change from the inside out. That said, the performance also has to work from the top down and energy and direction also have to come from the outside in.

- Each scene engaged multiple senses, and sequences employed multiple media. Dramatization was used to turn a meeting into an experience. One way to describe the team leader outbreaks and all-staff Learning Conferences is as "happenings."

- There was appeal to both the head and heart. This was expressed as the need to affect both the mindsets and heartsets of people. Physical activity and reflective moments, in turn, incorporated attention to body and soul.

In the end, it was clear that VdBN's brand of change-as-theater—from the warehouse wake-up call and orange hat skating promotion to the team leader gathering in the Ardennes and the learning history extravaganza in the Jordanian desert—transformed both individuals and teams and left an enormous imprint on an entire company. But to judge its lasting significance, never mind the particular elements that made it work so well here, is a matter of looking at a larger picture—the artful combination of certain processes and practices that we call "holistic integration."

Chapter 16

Holistic Integration

Describing how we achieved double-digit growth is
not easy. Only a holistic view will do. It is about
paradoxes: planning and luck, teams and
individuals, great ideas and small steps, far-reaching
ambition and everyday realism, being bold and
humble, through chaos and organization. Maybe we
can say it was "passion for winning."
            —*Marijn van Tiggelen, Commercial director*

This transformation story is not reducible to the models or methods
of change cited here, however important they may be. Nor can it
be replicated by simply staging and leading change as a performance, however artful a leader may be. Rather, it was the holistic
integration of elements—processes and performances, activity top
down and bottom up, energy inside out and outside in, changes
hard and soft—that drove the transformation of VdBN. Listing at
least some of these integrative points—*as they were known, talked
about, and incorporated into practice at VdBN*—may help in understanding what happened in this case and applying the lessons.

Personal *and* Business Growth

The drive for growth was an animating force at both UVGN and
VdBN. In each case, management's prior emphasis had been mostly
on profitability. Corporate appeals to shareholder value and the
threat of factory closures put growth on the agenda. What people

needed to internalize it was to see a link between business and personal growth. There was a pragmatic argument joining the two: top-line growth provides job security and career opportunities. In time, the message that growth creates excitement, challenge, and meaning evolved; it was simply more fun to grow a business.

Listen to this factory floor team leader, who has written down his lessons about growth in newfound business terms:

> Today many people in VdBN make a connection between business and personal growth. They argue that you have to grow people to grow a business. And that growing a business stimulates personal growth. This logic justified a wide range of significant investments in personal and organizational development in the belief that spending money in these areas would pay off. Second, it translated into stretch targets for people as well as the business. An expectation emerged that your job was to improve yourself.

And listen to this sales director mix management-speak into casual talk about the human dimensions of growth:

> A young woman, who was still in school four years ago, now has a budget of 150 million guilders. She leads the business; she has got her own team. The funny thing is that they feel the need to talk and all of sudden this really close account team emerges, because they need each other as sparring partners or for benchmarking to achieve something together. You see a brilliant team emerging. They say that themselves as well: "I have never worked in such a great team before." Of course, I coach, and give them direction, but they have to do it themselves. And that is great, because you see that you really empower people like that.

Head *and* Heart

The idea of connecting head and heart evolved over the five years. In strategic reviews, with the emphasis on business thinking, analyses of the marketplace, and attention to customers and competition, the intention was to upgrade business *mindsets* in the company. A combination of more open and personal communication among team leaders and staff, the spread of Covey training, and interest in emotional intelligence and its applications underscored the value of changing *heartsets* as well.[1]

This emphasis on head and heart had the immediate benefit of validating the more emotive, right-brain types in the company and what they had to contribute. "I am really happy with the change in the last five years. The company now relies more on emotions," noted a design director. "I am creative. I am somebody who works out of his feelings. They trust me and know my feelings are reliable and good."

It also expanded the range of ideas and repertoire of human relations in the company:

> *From a safety manager:* When I came here the balance was extremely on the logical side. But sometimes it's very difficult for a manager to say, "I'm planning this and this will be the result." It makes such a difference when you hear a bit of emotion like, "I trust you. I don't see the result yet but I trust you'll do the right thing, so go ahead!"

> *From a marketing manager:* Some of the crazy ones we had in our group—the ones who made it happen—are the kinds of people that normally wouldn't be successful in Unilever. And they turned out to be the best people you could think of. I was extremely pleased that we spent so much time and effort in the emotional part of developing. We have a more balanced group of people.

The link between head and heart was felt at every layer of the pyramid of growth. For individuals, it was a means, as one described it, to "connect to self." Neil Wickers, the former GM in Fats, demonstrated this self-understanding movingly when he presented the person-behind-the-mask to everyone in VdBN at an annual learning conference. "Unilever has been an extremely strong company for analytical people like me," he commented later. "With exercises like we did, you start to build much more understanding about yourself, which I find extremely positive." Said another manager, "There was a level of introspection, of thinking about what's going on inside, about reactions to what's going on and to each other." In a broader sense, this emphasis on self-knowledge was about discovering the whole person and bringing that wholeness into work.[2]

For teams, it was a means to "connect to others."[3] This was of course the need and aspiration that emerged in the management meeting in Antwerp in 1997, when managers from the newly merged UVGN and VdBN saw clips from the movie *The Abyss* and wept together over their lack of connection to one another. "It helped people to connect in their minds," recalled one, "and to connect in their hearts." The subsequent launch of team leader events and construction of a communal work area cum café laid the groundwork for a new kind of human organization to take shape.[4] Said Gerard Prins, "There is now an interconnection between people. I know you better and I know who you are. I have heard you talking at meetings and thought, 'Well, that's an idea I like.' I can call you and talk with you. We have in fact been building a community."

For the organization and business, the link between head and heart had relevance as well. "We tended to be very much business-oriented, with focus on business systems, procedures, policies, strategies and so on," remarked one manager. To balance this side, there was a complementary emphasis on theatrics, outdoor adventure, and playfulness. This was expressed both inside the company and in making connections to retail customers and consumers. It entered into managerial practice. Said one marketer, "I found the ability to move an organization, in fact, the ability to move a market, through a lucid, convincing, and consistent story that is well told. I found out that I could be a storyteller, or the editor writing the story with others." The criteria for judging the success of communications, meetings, and events were twofold: "Is it intellectually convincing? Is it emotionally appealing?"

Outside In *and* Inside Out

Much of the commercial success of VdBN came from turning good ideas into winning value propositions. Many of these ideas came from the outside in. For example, the Foods business studied the market and consumption trends, visited company canteens and on-the-go eating spots, hosted countless focus groups, and benchmarked other businesses to develop new product and distribution ideas. Fats looked more closely at consumer mindsets and engaged retail customers en masse on the Big Night. Countless consultants brought in outside information and expertise—about strategy and marketing for the business units, and about TPM and teaming for the factories. Books on the latest thinking in business were distributed widely and tracts on existential philosophy and psychology were perused. All of this expanded the gene pool of ideas in the company and reinforced the point, made early and often, that leaders were expected to be "students of business and leadership."

At the same time, there was a complementary emphasis on taking action based on personal insight, intuition, and conviction. Recall the young marketer in Foods who said, "The learning for me in this whole process was how important intuition and daring are to success. . . . in the end it is not only about one plus one is two. It's about what you believe in." Outside experts and market research argued against the relaunch of Uno Noodles, the Blue Band cookbook promotion, and several other innovations introduced by VdBN. On these counts, business leaders were successful because they listened to their people and to their instincts.

Nowhere was the value of operating from the inside out more important than in leadership. In management studies, it wasn't too long ago that situational leadership was in vogue and leaders were advised to adapt their style to the characteristics of the situation.[J] At VdBN, by comparison, the teaching through principles and parables, the emphasis on self-reflection, and the use of "I" statements in conversation all carried a different message about leadership at

VdBN: forget about what the textbooks say, leadership here is about authenticity, vulnerability, and just being yourself.

Top Down *and* Bottom Up

In many respects, the transformation of VdBN was led from the top down—by the chairman overall and by young leaders in their business and sourcing units. The mechanisms, familiar to business leaders and change agents, involved *replication* and *cascading*. Certainly the change methods introduced in the first transformation (UVGN) were replicated in the second (VdBN). Efforts to signal urgency and mobilize people for change were similar in the two cases—albeit more intense in the first (with the warehouse wake-up call) and more encompassing in the second (with 180 team leaders in charge). Organizational change methods, in turn, were learned by business and team leaders who replicated them as they cascaded the approach down into the organization.

While this was very much a top-down approach to transformation, two other dynamics helped institutionalize and, in a sense, democratize the capacity to produce change in the company. First, the cascade model helped to develop "leadership at every level."[6] The sequence of first participating in a change step and then leading it in their work area built a base of experience and self-confidence among leaders. In time, the factories and business units launched their own local versions of the leadership outbreaks and company-wide learning conferences. Second, many work teams learned the language and methods of organizational change, and applied them to their particular problems and needs—the discipline of team learning.[7]

There also were instances in VdBN when practices developed in lower levels rose "bottom up" and influenced the company overall. Geert Maassen's early success with teaming in the Nassaukade factory and his gutsy trip to the Sinai are two examples. The exchange of ideas and models between Foods and Fats is another illustration of change flowing through the business rather than from the top down. But the real counterbalance to top-down pressure to change was the sense of freedom and autonomy that many people experienced in their transformed work environments. Most often this was expressed in terms of space: "You create space, give people room to develop, give them room to run the business as they like," said one marketing executive, "that was a big success factor."

The importance of space was one of the subtle themes of the VdBN story. Gunning talked about creating a space where people could reflect and combine their intellect and emotion. Many others spoke about value of having space to think, to talk deeply with others, to innovate, to make mistakes, and to learn from them. In a metaphysical sense, however, opening up space—intellectual, emotional, physical and spiritual—also meant giving up control of transformation. Indeed there was widespread recognition that upheaval and confusion were essential to the process. Listen to one sales service manager's view of what happened:

> I don't know exactly. I thought that it was a little bit engineered at the beginning and then the genie was out of the bottle and not under control anymore. A complete engineered picture at the start, then let's create chaos.

Order *and* Chaos

The idea that companies succeed by simultaneously balancing order and chaos is not new; it was first popularized in management circles in the 1980s with *In Search of Excellence* in its critique of the "rational model" and emphasis on managing paradox through, for example, the pairing of loose-and-tight. It has been elaborated since in organization theory, strategy, and transformational management.[8] The adaptive process involves reckoning with paradoxes posed in business—between, say, planning and luck, teams and individuals, great ideas and small steps, far-reaching ambition and everyday realism, as VdBN's commercial director put it; and it means being both bold and humble, and integrating both chaos and organization.

The new science of organization and leadership puts this into models of "complex adaptive systems" and speaks to practice in terms of self-organizing or, more popularly, surfing at the edge of chaos.[9] Interestingly, the arts have their own understandings and language about order and chaos. Jamming in jazz music, improvisation in the theater, or jujitsu in the martial arts all exemplify balance and integration.[10] Needless to say, complementary ideas can be found in literature and poetry, in the creative arts and scientific discovery, and in sports and medicine.[11] These core ideas and applications populate the business management section of the bookstore today.

There is also "ancient" wisdom on these matters.[12] Notions of an unseen order can be found in Buddhist tracts and Western faith and in indigenous people's understandings of the world. The rising interest in spirituality in business attests to the appeal of this kind of knowledge and talk about synchronicity and transcendence is not uncommon in change management circles nowadays.[13] The central idea is that we live in a naturally and gracefully evolving universe. Change is about creating a space in which it can unfold.

These ideas from science, art, and spirituality found their way into the transformation at VdBN. Some came in via books and outside experts—the latest thinking in strategy, the reflections of existential philosophy, the writings of M. Scott Peck, the Covey and FCE consultants, and countless other management books, articles, and talks. Some bubbled up in references to sports, the arts, and literature, and some from reflections on personal experiences at events and in the workplace. Understandings about order and chaos, integration and balance, can be found throughout this transformation story. Gunning talked in terms of managing intangibles:

> What people seem to miss in their philosophy of leadership, in their vision, in their implementing of change, is the managing of intangibles. You can work on people's intellect, and on people's emotions, but you want to integrate these at continuously higher levels. You always build on your previous move. And you always try to come to

higher levels of integration. That is the cumulative effect of events, of applying principles, of walking your talk, and being consistent in your beliefs. It is the integration of these intangibles that makes the difference.

Others talked about this in terms of creating magic. And still others of creating space for miracles.

Postscript

When Gunning first met with Mirvis in 1998, he was in search of a tested model to develop teams and deepen the sense of community in the company. That first encounter launched an ongoing struggle about whether in fact "miracles" could be designed. Gunning initially wanted a cookbook for building community because he'd gotten a cookbook from Covey. There were a number of back-and-forths about how predictable a full-scale transformation was, could, or even should be.

Our emphasis on the artful combination of practices, or "holistic integration," as key to success is no doubt agreeable to experienced managers. But the research yielded no "models" on holistic practice—at least none that would yield predictable results. It is at best speculative how artful actions connect causally to changes in people's attitudes, behaviors, and business results. And commentary on the role of synchronicity or spirituality in the transformation is best left to the people who led and participated in the change. In any case, it is foolish to assume that any of the practices documented can be applied in a "cookbook" fashion. As Gunning later remarked, "I have tried the cookbook. It doesn't work."

Marking progress and creating change in organizations via events is still a new idea. Nonetheless, we have some conclusions about what was most essential to the success here:

- In "producing" change: A mix of planning and improvisation that led to timely action allowing the desired change to unfold

- In "*performing*" *change:* Intense and profound engagement in the change process, as individuals and as a community
- In "*experiencing*" *change:* Creating space and allowing serendipity to work

As to the overall significance of the performative events, the jury is out and must remain so. Certainly the notion that organization change follows nonlinear, unpredictable directions is not a novel conclusion.[14] Nor is the idea that to understand and appreciate such patterns, it helps to turn to nontraditional forms of assessment, such as the storytelling you've heard here.[15] The methods of literary and theater critics, and of performing art scholarship more generally, would perhaps provide a more analytic and rigorous rendering of the aesthetic dimensions of VdBN's transformation.

When we assess this transformation as an art form that has engaged and changed a community of people, however, it seems less appropriate to use these tools or to try to tease out the key elements that made it work. As when looking at a painting, we could attend to details such as brush strokes, lighting, colors, and shapes, or focus on the arrangement of the canvas and its framing, but in the end, what matters first and foremost is how the painting as a whole strikes the viewer. In his commentary on the validity of art, Michael Polanyi observed that its "truth" lay in the *experience* it creates for those who see the artwork or, in this case, participated in the transformation.[16]

The learning history was both a part of and a contributor to the transformation of VdBN. When performing, actors tend to take on and become their roles, and with artistic license dramatize and orient themselves for the effect of it all. Certainly this concern was with us as researchers when we heard rapturous accounts of the Ardennes or watched evocative videos of other meaningful events in the company's transformational timeline.[17] In so doing, we would check for bias by probing into people's positive experiences about events and challenge them to show us demonstrable results of their impact. At the same time, the goal of helping people to look inward, backward, and forward to learn from experience is one that we identified with and tried to bring about. Thus our probing and challenging had less to do with objectifying the experience for academic purposes and more to do with advancing the learning agenda on site.

Let us be straightforward on these counts: Not all aspects of the performances at VdBN, including the time in Jordan, were intellectually, emotionally, or aesthetically compelling. There were flops. As producer and director, Gunning had his own failings and, as he has said here, his performance was not always on the mark. Of greater concern going forward has been his central role in the transformation. We wonder whether change management by performance is possible without a compelling and theatrical individual in charge.

In many companies, planned change processes seem rote and the experience is grinding and ultimately defeating. Adding performativity to the change process at VdBN made it more playful, meaningful, and ultimately rewarding.[18] One indication of the validity of this approach is that select team leaders at VdBN began to stage learning performances for their own businesses and teams. We hope leaders in other companies can carry performativity even further.

Appendix 1:
Cast of Characters
—Then and Now

The story draws from the history books created by all the eighteen hundred employees of VdBN—now renamed Unilever Bestfoods (UBF)—in February 2000 and interviews with over a hundred people who worked at UVGN or VdBN from 1995 to 2000, others from Unilever senior ranks and those organizational consultants, retailers, advertising agencies, and other outsiders who have worked closely with VdBN. As this is literally a cast of thousands we can't possibly name them all. The roster below lists the main characters featured in the book—where they were then and where they are now.

	Then (1995–2000)	*Now (2003)*
Adriaan Bertens	FCE Consultant, Netherlands	Independent consultant
Evert Bos	Brand manager, UVGN/VdBN	CRM manager, Netherlands
Conny Braams	Category manager Fats, VdBN	SCC Marketing/ BU director, UBF
Antony Burgmans	Cochairman, Unilever	Same
Jose Cavanna	Consultant, Proudfoot	Independent consultant
Hans Cornuit	HR director, UVGN/VdBN	HR director, de Goudse

Albert Desaunois	Union steward, Nassaukade	Same
Roef van Duin	Plant manager, Royco	Plant manager, Nassaukade
Kees Ekelmans	Finance director, UVGN/VdBN	UBF
Rein Ettema	Chief engineer, UVGN/VdBN	Plant manager, Oss (Unox factories)
Mick van Ettinger	Director, Uniquisine, VdBN	Director Foods, UBF Vietnam
Niall Fitzgerald	Cochairman, Unilever	Same
Tex Gunning	Chairman, UVGN/VdBN	President, UBF Asia
Ann Hoewing	FCE Consultant, USA	Independent consultant
Jaap Kalma	Marketing manager Fats, VdBN	Director Foods, UBF Italy
Alex Korbee	Company physician, VdBN	Same
Kees Kruythoff	Marketing manager, VdBN	UBF Asia
Ankie van Lindt	Team trainer, Royco	Team trainer, UBF
Geert Maassen	Team leader and trainer, Nassaukade	Retired
Hans Mikkelsen	Sales director Foods, VdBN	Same
Ad van Oers	Plant manager, Calvé	Supply chain director, UBF Vietnam

Arjan Overwater	Senior VP	Human Resources, Unilever HQ
Jeff Pitt	The Learning Company, U.K.	Deceased
Gerard Prins	E-commerce manager, VdBN	Same
Eric Jan de Rooij	Partner, Multi-Level Travel	Same
Bauke Rouwers	Marketing director Foods, VdBN	Vice president, Lipton Foods UBF North America
Hans van't Sant	Department head and trainer, VdBN	Retired
David Saunders	Covey consultant	Independent consultant
Rob Schaerlaeckens	HR manager, UVGN/VdBN	Liptonice, UBF Vietnam
Leon Schoofs	Sales director Fats, VdBN	Retired
Janti Soeripto	Finance director Fats, VdBN	SCC Finance/BU director, UBF
Anthonie Stal	EVP Culinary, Unilever	Chairman, UBF Netherlands
Hein Swinkels	Chief accountant, UVGN	Director, UBF Netherlands
Hans Synhaeve	Manufacturing director, UVGN/VdBN	Regional sourcing director, Unilever HQ
Marijn van Tiggelen	Commercial director Foods, VdBN	Senior VP, UBF South East Asia

Aart-Jan (AJ) van Triest	Marketing director Fats, VdBN	VP Marketing Knorr, UBF Asia
Neil Wickers	General manager Fats, VdBN	Director, UBF, SCC Category
John Zealy	Andersen consultant	Consultant

Appendix 2: Learning History

> This interview is for the learning history. So it is
> meant for understanding and learning from the
> past. But I can only tell you things from my
> perspective, how I see them through my glasses.
> Perhaps it's not *the* truth, but it's my truth.
>
> —*Account manager*

Learning from experience is something that every individual does
naturally. We think and act to achieve our goals, and then rethink,
react, and regroup when we find out that our efforts have not been
successful. But as individuals we aren't perfect learners. Many factors that we are not aware of affect our performance. We aren't always so thorough or systematic about connecting objectives, actions,
and outcomes that we can test and refine our understandings of how
things work. And our drives to make the world more understandable
often lead us to develop overly simple rules of thumb for complex situations. For these reasons, interest in how we can learn *collectively* is
increasing—hence the interest in organizational learning.

Research into organizational learning has focused on describing, developing, and testing conditions that support collective
learning. One such effort, developed initially to capture and diffuse
what can be learned from managing change, involves the creation
of a learning history. The product of a learning history is a document that is developed through a consultation and research process.
The document is a retrospective history of significant events in a
company's recent past, described in the voices of people who took

part in them. Researched through reflective interviews and quote-checked scrupulously, the learning history relies on storytelling to help a company evaluate and accelerate its progress in learning (see Exhibit A2.1).

The learning history methodology was invented by George Roth and Art Kleiner to help close the gap between action and reflection, or between leading change and learning from it.[1] It tells an organization its own story. Deliberately presented in an engaging

Exhibit A2.1 Learning from Stories and History

Organizational history, made up of the experiences of employees' and the firm's performance, is an importance source of learning. While visioning, strategy, and planning processes push a firm forward, history anchors it. Many companies muddle along because they disregard the insights of past lessons. What made for past success is not understood and cannot be replicated; instead mistakes are repeated. Managers prefer to develop visions for better futures without examining the current and historical realities that led to present conditions. Firms do not create their desired future from neutral places. The distance between what is desired and where they are is the territory that a firm needs to cover knowingly. The effort, energy, and change that managers and firms muster to achieve their desired future will be inadequate if they fail to account for historical forces. Like an anchor, history is a source of competence and stability that can also be a drag on new efforts.

Learning histories are part of a process that engages an organization to consider a critical event or an improvement initiative. The process produces a jointly told, retrospective account of significant events. The document presents the experiences of people in their own words. The contents come from the people who initiated, implemented, participated in, and were affected by the effort. Quotes from interviews are edited and woven together to produce an account of what happened, that account being told from different perspectives.

The document is used as an artifact from which conversations in new groups can take place on what happened, why it happened, how it applies to them, and how they can improve their future action. Then, in creating settings where people read, discuss, and reflect about others in an effort to help them think, plan, and act for themselves, we recreate an experience for them. The experience is organizational—in its telling through interviews, production by an insider-outsider team of historians, validation by going back to check quotes and their use in context, and its reception in reading and discussion sessions.

fashion, this story is intended to stimulate conversations that capture and permeate an organization with learning. The narrative flow of the document calls to mind a conversation among friends—a group of people sitting around a living room, each with a different piece of the narrative to offer.[2]

In putting together a learning history, its creators keep three imperatives in mind:

- *The research imperative:* Staying true to the data (so that everything in the document is recognized as valid)

- *The mythic imperative:* Staying true to the story (so that the text captures people's attention)

- *The pragmatic imperative:* Staying true to the audience (so that it is cast in a way that helps a organization learn and move forward)

Innovations in Learning History

One thing that made the learning history of VdBN distinctive was the effort to integrate it directly into the transformation of the business. It was designed to help everyone in the company to surface and test their understandings about past actions and incorporate them into their future efforts. "I have only been team leader for a short while now and I felt like I was missing bits and pieces," said one team leader prior to the trip to Jordan. "I found it challenging to become part of this group." Afterward, he remarked, "I really notice the difference. I really want to learn from this history. I will commit myself for 200 percent. As a team leader, I envision loads of challenges both for my team and for the company."

The second distinctive feature was, of course, the staging and setting of the team leaders' learning review. For the past several years, VdBN managers had traveled afar to talk business and share personal stories. But the magnificence and significance of the program in the desert was unmatched by prior experiences. The first day of the program, for example, included a visit to the old city of Jerusalem—a place of such significance that the importance and sensation of its history is overt and palpable to all who walk there today. Over the course of the team leaders' event, people passed by Masada (where the Jews held out against King Herod) and the caves of Qumran (where the Dead Sea Scrolls were discovered). We met in Wadi Rum (where Lawrence of Arabia gathered Bedouin tribes) and climbed a mountain to descend into the Nabataean civilization of Petra (where the valley of sandstone cliffs is etched with the facades of the great architectural styles of Egypt, Greece, and Rome). Western civilization has been shaped by the history that comes from this setting. The choice of these learning locales was no accident; it made questions about how history shapes you very real and memorable.

To prepare for the Jordan event, the team leaders had each reflected on their personal history with VdBN by preparing a timeline of key personal and business experiences. Later, nestled into the mountainside, talking, arguing, sometimes laughing, sometimes tearful, they shared these experiences, the highs and lows, and their own learning from the past five years. Work units created banners that highlighted their most meaningful experiences from 1995 to 2000. They then reported them to other teams around a roaring campfire. The wind was still, the talk was careful, and the listening was intense. Everyone understood that they were not only learning from history, they were making it.

During the next three days, in discussions on rocky cliffs, while walking or riding in Jeeps, and by firesides in the desert, team leaders cycled between individual and collective consideration of their history, the lessons, and needed actions and plans. These conversations were surely influenced by travel to a locale far from home, by being together amid geologic beauty and historic significance, and by living close as to nature as a Bedouin tribe.

The scale and scope of creating the learning history involving the whole of VdBN was also unique. Following their trip to the desert, team leaders took their insights and learning back to the organization. The company-wide Learning Conference 2000, set in a warehouse renovated for company conventions, engaged eighteen hundred total in the company in reviewing past experiences and identifying future implications. People shared their history lines and stories and listened as each of their teammates did the same. Based on the highs and lows, each team then constructed its own collective history line and prepared a logbook of breakthrough stories; 180 of these team history books were created, covering key events, lessons from the past, and visions for the future.

Preparing the Learning History

The history lines, breakthrough stories, and history books were only part of the input to the VdBN learning history. In parallel to retreats and events, researchers and a small team of people inside the company interviewed key individuals and led discussions with workgroups (see Exhibit A2.2).

The sources of data for the learning history included the following:

- Interviews and focus groups with VdBN managers and staff and with other executives and consultants who have worked with the company (over 120 in all).

Exhibit A2.2 Learning History Process for VdBN

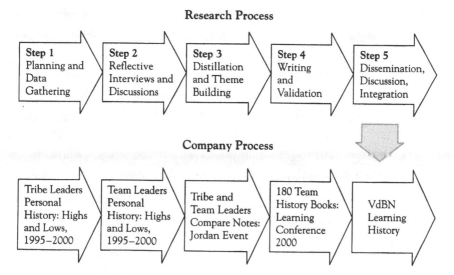

Research Process

| Step 1
Planning and Data Gathering | Step 2
Reflective Interviews and Discussions | Step 3
Distillation and Theme Building | Step 4
Writing and Validation | Step 5
Dissemination, Discussion, Integration |

Company Process

| Tribe Leaders Personal History: Highs and Lows, 1995–2000 | Team Leaders Personal History: Highs and Lows, 1995–2000 | Tribe and Team Leaders Compare Notes: Jordan Event | 180 Team History Books: Learning Conference 2000 | VdBN Learning History |

- Preparation of "history lines" and reviews of breakthrough experiences that were created for and summarized in the February 2000 team leaders' event in Jordan.
- Personal and business breakthrough stories by all VdBN employees shared at the 2000 Learning Conference.
- Audio- and videotapes, copies of presentations, and background reports of various management meetings.
- Discussions with Tex Gunning, the internal learning history team, consultants, and others in VdBN about the events and findings.
- Our own experience, notes, and records from participating in some of the events.

The learning history, used by VdBN and others in Unilever, was rewritten into this book to tell this story of transformation to a broader audience.

Data and Themes

The breakthroughs reported in team history books were often quite moving (see Exhibit A2.3). Among the business achievements cited were successful product launches, factory improvements, organizational changes, and team accomplishments. Personal breakthroughs were equally compelling. They were traced to mentoring, participation in team leader events and training, Covey courses, and everyday personal development.

Part of our job, as researchers and observers, was to organize these breakthrough stories and conceptualize what happened at VdBN into central themes (see Exhibit A2.4). The chronological story of transformation in VdBN was punctuated by several action cycles—each with its own characteristics. For instance, the turnaround in UVGN commenced with a dramatic call to action to "prevent the ship from sinking." Then people were mobilized to grow volume and regain market share, a phase labeled "building the business."

Exhibit A2.3 Sample Breakthroughs

Business Breakthrough

In the first quarter of '99, we experienced the sweet taste of a step-change in performance. We all discussed the state Calvé was in. It was easy to see where we would end up if we continued the trend through the year. This created a sense of urgency and we focused on critical success factors in production to be able to show improvement ASAP.

Due to this focus, there was no gap between conceptual ideas and the priorities of operators. Many improvement ideas came bottom up due to our culture change—fewer layers, open and informal atmosphere. People communicating ideas were heard and understood. By our "shareholder day," all negative trends had turned positive: a step-change in efficiency, less waste versus the norm, and A-status quality, and good levels of cleanliness.

The lesson I learned is that you will not achieve step-change by debating it or preparing for a long time. You should look for big hits, agree to focus on them, and then just start and follow up. As soon as you have shared some successes, the agenda on what to do next will be filled with good ideas. Now it is regarded as normal that everybody volunteers to drive a part of the agenda.

Personal Breakthrough

During the last years I realized that in working with people it's not about who is right or wrong. What counts is building working relationships with people to achieve that "end-in-mind." I learned to choose my battles more wisely, to value personal differences more, and got a sixth-sense for where the other person is coming from.

My development was very intense because:

1. I worked in a team where "being yourself" was a prerequisite.
2. My (boss) created "space" and showed trust in me.
3. My colleagues and I evaluated ourselves on almost a continuous basis (what are our roles, honestly/vulnerably telling how irritating we each sometimes were, feedback on how to improve, etc.).

My lessons for the future:

1. Only in a safe environment where leadership on different levels is sincere and professional can people really be themselves, challenge issues, take initiatives. This brings out the best in people.
2. The emotionally appealing parts of leadership should be valued as much as the intellectually convincing parts.
3. Bosses should be coaches. This requires sincere interest in personal development and continuous feedback in an honest way.

This cycle was repeated following the merger with VdBN—"A new beginning." The combined company intent was "competing for the future." In subsequent years attention was given respectively to building community (inside the company) and to reconnecting with customers and consumers (outside the firm).

The team leaders' event in February 2000 marked the start of a new transformation cycle where people were asked to face the challenges of the new economy and the torch passed to a new leader for VdBN. Our research identified, for each of these cycles, material on the following:

- The key theme each year in the transformation
- The management process used to effect change
- The key events or performances that dramatized change
- The symbols used to convey the meaning and significance of the period
- The specific "hard" and "soft" changes introduced
- The company's current examples of holistic integration

Tracking these details across the cycles of transformation suggests that VdBN leaders had, over this period, been learning to proactively manage change. The connection between the soft work of developing people and the organization with the hard numbers of financial and market measures was not always direct and visible in each period. However, when viewed over time, the link between development and results is in our view convincing and compelling.

To the "Outside World"

This learning history effort was also aimed at the outside world, especially for managers, change agents, and students. It is our hope that they find the research story credible, the mythic story motivating, and the pragmatic story useful. And we encourage others to consider how to design a learning performance wherein the making of a learning history is itself a history-making event.

Exhibit A2.4 Transformation Themeline

Transformation Themes	Preventing the Ship from Sinking	Building the Business	Merging: A New Beginning	Competing for the Future	Community: Deepen Passion for Growth	Reconnecting: Grow Together	Passing the Torch
Timeframe	1995	1996–1997	1997	1997	1998	1999	2000
Management Process	Wake-Up I: Face Reality	Vision: Grow x 2; Mobilize	Wake-Up II: Face Market	Vision: Legacy of Growth	Cascade: 180 Team Leaders	Replicate: We all have to contribute	Wake-Up III: Reinvent yourself
Key Events or Performances	Warehouse of Waste; 1400 people on 40 buses	MBO letter: Fix or sell; Unox Learning Conference; Skating event	VdBN goes into therapy; Learning Conference 97—2000 points of light	Revolution in Foods: Management Conference—The Abyss	Ardennes offensive: Learning Conference 98—Teams make the difference	Scotland: McVan den Bergh clans; Big Night for Customers	Jordan: Learn from the past; Learning Conference 2000; Big Night II
Symbols	Stacks of bad food pallets; Bulldozer burial; Old must die	New tricks—Juggling; Unox hats on skaters; Dive into sea; Rebirth	Vulnerable volume; Trust falls, Breaking boards, Party	Planet VdBN logo; Index 100 targets	Cynics versus believers; Emotional lifelines; Board fishbowl	Flags and songs; Young leaders and teams take charge	Tribes in Petra; New leader takes the torch
"Hard" Change	Layoffs and delayering; Business thinking	Profit-and-Loss responsibility: TPM program begins	Strategic review	Organization review; Stretch goals; Scratch quality	Business Units: Value Creation and Value Delivery	Growing Market with Foods; Growing Share with Fats; Sourcing Units: Costs and Quality	
"Soft" Change	Hands-on engagement; Informal style	Teaching and inspiring; Young leaders	Countering the culture clash	Spread of Seven Habits; Angry young men	Team training and community building	Missionary Work: Circle of disciples implements vision	"I am leaving, you can do it."
Holistic Integration	Creative destruction	Empower/Disempower	Changing mindsets; Changing heartsets			Organized chaos	Back to the future

Notes and Sources

Preview: The View from the Desert

1. Opening epigraph and passage quoted here from T. E. Lawrence, *Seven Pillars of Wisdom: A Triumph* (New York: Anchor Books, 1991), pp. 350–351. (Originally published 1935.)

2. Unilever is one of Europe's biggest businesses, with total sales for 2002 of almost €52 billion, and total operating profits of just over €4.2 billion. Its corporate centers are London and Rotterdam. The two parent companies, Unilever NV and Unilever PLC, together with their group companies, operate "as nearly as practicable as a single entity" (*Unilever Annual Review 2002 and Summary Financial Statement*, p. 1). For more on Unilever's history and current status, see http://www.unilever.com.

3. Dutch sensitivity to embarrassment is a long-standing cultural characteristic. On its sociocultural sources, and for more on the rich tapestry of Dutch culture, see Simon Schama, *The Embarrassment of Riches: An Interpretation of Dutch Culture in the Golden Age* (New York: Vintage, 1997).

4. The words of everyone "on the record" come from tape-recorded interviews with some 120 VdBN managers and staff, plus other executives and consultants who worked with the company. We also had a database of nearly 1800 people's personal and business breakthrough stories, plus work team "history books" (over 150 in all) to work with.

Chapter 1

1. "Tex" has nothing to do with Texas or being a "cowboy." It is a family nickname derived from the name of a great-uncle's sailing ship, *Den Tex*.
2. Howard Gardner reviews several studies that document how future leaders have lost fathers at an early age in *Leading Minds* (New York: HarperCollins, 1995). James McGregor Burns, in *Leadership* (New York: Harper and Row, 1978), reports that Ghandi and Lenin, among many other disparate types of leaders, had a positive relationship with one parent and negative relationship with the other. Michael Csikszentmihalyi, in *The Evolving Self* (New York: HarperCollins, 1993), finds defiance of authority a common trait of leaders-to-be, and Sigmund Freud analyzed self-reliance in the face of opposition in *Group Psychology and the Analysis of the Ego, Standard Edition* (London: Hogarth Press, 1955), 18: 69–143.
3. Among Tex's favored books, passed out to colleagues, were *Man's Search for Meaning* by Victor Emil Frankl (New York: Pocket Books, 1976) and *Art of Loving* by Erich Fromm (New York: HarperCollins, 2000); also M. Scott Peck's *Road Less Traveled: A New Psychology of Love, Traditional Values and Spiritual Growth*, 25th anniv. ed. (New York: Simon & Schuster, 2002).
4. After a decade and a half of restructuring, reengineering, and downsizing, leading U.S.-based companies had by the mid-1990s significantly reduced their overhead, modernized factories, and focused squarely on performance. Some large firms such as General Electric and Coca-Cola had boosted growth to the point that they would compete favorably during the boom of high-tech and dot-com companies.

    By the mid-1990s, Europe-based companies, including British Telecom, Lufthansa, ABB, British Petroleum, and Royal Dutch Shell, had embarked on their transformations. In what the *Economist* (November 1996) still characterized as a "fortress against change," these European firms began to resize and re-shape themselves, expand their offerings, and change long-standing work practices and traditional social contracts with their employees and communities. The emergence of global media, markets, brands, and products, the primacy given to share-holder interests, and the advances in technology and changes in consumer attitudes and tastes were all stimulants to change in these firms.

Chapter 2

1. The strategy consultants were from Andersen Consulting, now Accenture. See http://www.accenture.com/.
2. Stephen Covey, *The Seven Habits of Highly Effective People* (New York: Simon & Schuster, 1989).
3. See, for example, Barbara Bunker and Billie Alban, *Large Group Interventions: Engaging the Whole System for Rapid Change* (San Francisco: Jossey-Bass, 1997); Dannemiller Tyson Associates, *Whole-Scale Change: Unleashing the Magic in Organizations* (San Francisco: Berrett-Koehler, 2000); Harrison Owen, *Open Space Technology: A User's Guide* (San Francisco: Berrett-Koehler, 1997).
4. See, for example, Peter M. Senge, *The Fifth Discipline: The Art and Practice of the Learning Organization* (New York: Currency Doubleday, 1990); Peter M. Senge and others, *The Fifth Discipline Fieldbook: Strategies and Tools for Building a Learning Organization* (New York: Currency Doubleday, 1994); and Peter M. Senge and others, *The Dance of Change: The Challenges to Sustaining Momentum in Learning Organizations* (New York: Doubleday, 1999).
5. Total Preventive Maintenance (TPM) is a way for people to work in teams to continuously improve operational effectiveness by eliminating losses of materials, time, and quality. The program embraces zero waste, dedication to detail, a systematic approach, and extensive training. The underlying objective is

to create an organization driven by teams. As with the well-known Japanese Total Quality Management programs, benefits came when the approach was embraced as part of a larger cultural change. The underlying objective was to create an organization driven by teams.

Chapter 3

1. Typically the lead unit in a merger, often larger and financially stronger, has studied the situation longer and developed a game plan. Its leaders are eager to move ahead and implement their plans. By comparison, the other party is generally a step behind analytically and emotionally unprepared to keep pace with rapid-fire decisions. As a result, the lead company's management often comes across as headstrong or arrogant, and managers of the to-be-merged firm are usually on the defensive. See Philip H. Mirvis and Mitchell L. Marks, *Managing the Merger*, 2nd ed. (Frederick, Md.: Beard Books, 2003). (Original edition published by Prentice Hall, 1992.)
2. See Mitchell L. Marks and Philip H. Mirvis, *Joining Forces: Making One Plus One Equal Two in Mergers, Acquisitions, and Alliances* (San Francisco: Jossey-Bass, 1997) on roots and implications of culture clashes.

Chapter 4

1. For the basics, see Sigmund Freud, *New Introductory Lectures on Psychoanalysis*, edited by J. Strachey (New York: Norton, 1965).
2. What emerged at VdBN was a new "story" about past performance, symbolized by the worrisome phrase "vulnerable volume." See, for example, Roger Martin, "Changing the Mind of the Corporation," *Harvard Business Review* (November-December 1993): 5–12; Jeanne M. Liedtka and John W. Rosen-

blum, "Shaping Conversations: Making Strategy, Making Change," *California Management Review* 39, no. 1 (1996): 141–157; Gordon Shaw, Robert Brown, and Philip Bromiley, "Strategic Stories: How 3M Is Rewriting Business Planning," *Harvard Business Review* (May-June 1998): 3–8.

3. The phrase "intellectually convincing and emotionally appealing," like other ideas incorporated into VdBN's thinking and language, comes from Gary Hamel and C. K. Prahalad, *Competing for the Future* (Boston: Harvard Business School Press, 1994), an influential book read by Gunning and his team.

   The new theme "competing for the future" appeared on VdBN hats, jackets, and promotional material at learning conferences. The existing company logo, a circle and two curved lines, was transformed into a futuristic image: Posters featured space-age men and women, wearing costumes with the several Unox and VdBN brands, marching through an other-worldly landscape, carrying the company banner of "planet Van den Bergh." A graphic artist and event planner helped to theme the 1997 and 1998 gatherings. She reported:

   "This was a merger. I thought it was a great idea to emulate the idea of *Star Trek*—bringing different kinds of people together to explore space. The circle I made into a planet. The poster had people from all of the factories and showed all their product logos. We are competing for the future. We are starting a journey and looking toward the future. The Christmas cards and everything communicated that all the factories and work sites were together, joined under the name Van den Bergh. The main reason was to brand it all and say, 'OK, we're all in this together.'"

4. Index 100 is a BHAG—referring to what management researchers Jim Collins and Jerry Porras call a "Big, Hairy, Audacious Goal." See James C. Collins and Jerry Porras, *Built to Last: Successful Habits of Visionary Companies* (New York: Harper-Business, 1994).

Chapter 5

1. "Us against them" is a common dynamic between the two sides in merging companies. It can linger months after a merger and create intergroup conflict in a business team. For a general treatment, see Clayton P. Alderfer, "An Intergroup Perspective on Group Dynamics." In *Handbook of Organizational Behavior*, edited by J. Lorsch (Englewood Cliffs, N.J.: Prentice Hall, 1966).

2. In looking at changes in UVGN and VdBN, the themes of death and rebirth emerge repeatedly. Psychologist Harry Levinson makes the point that all change involves loss. Before a new way is accepted, old ways must die. In dealing with the loss, people progress from initial denial and anger to "bargaining," perhaps in the form of half-measures or promises to do better, and eventually accepting and coming to terms with loss to accept change. The pain of loss is lessened by the promise of rebirth and a hope for a brighter future. Harry Levinson, "Easing the Pain of Personal Loss," *Harvard Business Review* 50 (1972): 80–88.

Chapter 6

1. M. Scott Peck, *The Different Drum: Community Making and Peace* (New York: Simon & Schuster, 1987). On the matter of the cookbook, Peck writes, "The community building process works so well in part because it is so remarkably lacking in formulas and always full of surprises as the hidden becomes known. If it is to be healthy, an organization, just like an individual, must be willing now and then to take a well-calculated risk." See Peck's *A World Waiting to Be Born: Civility Rediscovered* (New York: Doubleday, 1993).

   Peck, among others, also theorizes about communities of leaders where everyone thinks and acts mindful of the whole. Rather then acting out of their own self-interest, leaders in such communities take careful account of others and reflect on their own feelings and needs. This leadership stresses the power inherent in deep communication and shared understanding among people. FCE stresses such principles in its training, including the importance of authentic communication, deep listening, and personal reflection. And it promotes certain practices—taking moments of silence, waiting to be moved to speak, and talking in a circle—that are often associated with meditative and spiritual traditions. In planning an event using these methods, there was naturally some trepidation about the mix of "inner" and "outer" work and about how the whole thing would play to a large group of team leaders.

2. As a technique for personal growth and team development, lifelines are used to help people to reflect on their background and share some of their personal life with colleagues to get to know one another more deeply. Originally developed by Herb Shepherd in the 1960s as a tool for life planning, they have since been used by many as a means to connect people in a group.

3. These basic components of Outward Bound–type programs allow teams to work on tasks that are different from their typical work place interactions. The activities are challenging and fun, and they build group management skills. Each exercise is reviewed and reflected upon in terms of the ways in which people support one another and contribute to a team effort. The insight and experience provide new approaches to team behavior that people can take back with them to their workplace.

4. The fishbowl is an approach developed in group dynamics research. It has people sitting in an inner circle debriefing their experience, while an outer circle looks on and learns from that experience. As part of the inner circle, the discussion of personal and group dynamics becomes the center of attention, and often the realization that there are onlookers learning drifts from awareness. That was what seemed to happen as the management board reflected on its teamwork and group dynamics.

Chapter 7

1. For an interesting comparison of attitudes of the Dutch to those of people from other parts of the world, see Fons Trompenaars and Charles Hampden-Turner, *Riding the Waves of Culture: Understanding Cultural Diversity in Global Business*, 2nd ed. (London: Nicholas-Brealey, 1997).

2. In his scholarly volume, *Leading Minds*, Howard Gardner emphasizes the importance of storytelling by leaders. The story reaches people intellectually and emotionally and puts their lives into a larger context. Consider: "The story is a basic human cognitive form; the artful creation and articulation of stories constitutes a fundamental part of the leader's vocation. Stories speak to both parts of the human mind—its reason and emotion."

   Gardner continues, "I deliberately use the terms story and narrative rather than message or theme. In speaking of stories, I want to call attention to the fact that leaders present a dynamic perspective to their followers: not just a headline or snapshot, but a drama that unfolds over time in which they—the leaders and followers—are the principal characters or heroes."

   Gardner particularly stresses the value of *identity stories*. Here the leaders reveal their characters and help followers to discover and develop their own identities. "It is the particular burden of the leader to help other individuals to determine their personal, social, and moral identities; more often than not, leaders inspire in part because of how they have resolved their own identity issues."

   Personal storytelling, whether in moments of reflection or in exercises like the emotional lifeline at VdBN, allow people to understand and connect to one another and in turn to connect themselves to a larger sphere of relationships and involvement. Note, however, that storytelling is not just talk—it is also walking the talk. See Howard Gardner, *Leading Minds* (New York: HarperCollins, 1995), and "Personal Histories: Leaders

Remember the Moments and People That Shaped Them,"
Harvard Business Review (December 2001): 3–11.

3. There are many factors to consider when contemplating community building in business. For instance, some employees
regard personal conversations of the sort found in community-
building workshops to be invasive of their privacy and feel a
subtle coercion to reveal something about their own private
lives. Furthermore, "loose talk" about spirituality, soul, and
other things sacred strikes some as inappropriate in a secular setting. It is crucial, therefore, to secure people's informed consent
before subjecting them to this kind of experience and to ensure
that they can opt out without prejudice or harm. It is also worth
noting that all manner of corporate consultants, helpers, and
healers are out there peddling their own variant of community
building and spiritual enrichment. The upshot? Buyer beware.

There is also potential danger when community feeling
takes hold in a business. The consciousness-raising can also be
called indoctrination. For instance, pundits went so far as to describe the heavy-handed socialization given employees at People Express as "Kool Aid Management," likening its demise to
Rev. Jim Jones's cult in Guyana, which ended in enforced mass
suicide. The introduction of spirituality into the mix raises the
stakes. There are, for example, documented cases of companies
that proselytize employees with specific religious doctrine. And
cases of corporate programs wherein employees exposed to
"New Age" ideas about consciousness and the cosmos felt their
own brand of faith compromised. Thus the tendency in public
education, as well as in most private venues, has been to erect a
wall between, say, church and state, faith and reason, spiritual
and secular matters of all kinds. Needless to say, this makes
thoughts and feelings about the spirit "undiscussable" in most
organizations.

On cautions, see Philip H. Mirvis, "Human Development
or Depersonalization: The Company of Total Community," in
The Fatal Embrace? edited by F. Heuberger and L. Nash (New

Brunswick, N.J.: Transaction, 1993); and Jay Conger, "Personal Growth Training: Snake Oil or Pathway to Leadership," *Organizational Dynamics* (Summer 1993): 19–30.

Chapter 8

1. This conversation after the trip to the mountain was conducted as a dialogue. In group dialogues, rather than debate a subject, participants are asked to inquire about assumptions, positions, and points of view rather than score points or even offer feedback. This reflective conversation, where everyone speaks to the group as a whole, creates space for what its practitioners describe as the "coherent movement of thought." The dialogue technique, as developed by William Isaacs and practiced by devotees of organizational learning, is particularly useful when a group is embroiled in conflict. Rather than take sides in the conflict, group members create a container that holds their differences up for inspection and keeps hot issues cooled sufficiently that people can explore their roots and ramifications. This facilitates development of group consciousness by counteracting tendencies toward *splitting* (where people identify with what they see as good parts of their group and reject the bad parts). On dialogue see William Isaacs, *Dialogue and the Art of Thinking Together: A Pioneering Approach to Communicating in Business and Life* (New York: Doubleday, 1999).

2. Here is where community-building principles apply. At the start of FCE-facilitated meetings, groundrules were set, for example, to "welcome and affirm diversity, deal with difficult issues, bridge differences with integrity, and relate with love and respect." Team leaders were advised that they could not lead their groups to community. But they and anyone else present could express their own thoughts, call for silence, or reflect on what was happening in the group. The intent was to create a "safe" environment for reflection.

    One community-building practice encourages people to "empty" themselves of thoughts and feelings that disconnect them from others. The famous fishbowl in the Ardennes was a first taste of "emptying" for many in the company. One year later, in Scotland, angry words after the tents collapsed and heartfelt talk about conflicts between work and family saw team leaders dealing with "difficult issues" with honest "I" statements about their discomfort and disagreements. This kind of talk, practiced in team-building sessions and circles of reflection, was carried over, in many instances, to everyday meetings where the subject might be products, performance, or people.

Community building is premised on the notion that people make community when they inquire into their *differences*, discover what they have in *common*, and then consciously embrace *unity*. See Philip H. Mirvis, "'Soul work' in organizations," *Organization Science* 8, no. 2 (1997): 193–206.

Chapter 9

1. For more on Boston Consulting Group, see http://www.bcg.com.
2. For more on these brands, see http://www.unilever.com.
3. Another influential book in VdBN at this time: Sumantra Ghoshal and Christopher A. Bartlett, *The Individualized Corporation: A Fundamentally New Approach to Management* (New York: HarperBusiness, 1997).
4. In analyzing their five-year learning history, the Foods business team identified a set of best practices in achieving breakthrough results. The practices included:

New Perspective:	From the "Outside In"
New Mindset:	Portfolio Analysis/Invest in Stars
New Concepts:	Food for Out of Home, On the Go
	Soups – Snacks
New Competitors:	Candy, Coffee, Tea
New Methods:	Multidisciplinary Account Teams
	Profit-and-Loss Responsibility
	Benchmarking (Heineken, Coca Cola)
	Bold Advertising and Promotions

Chapter 10

1. The Blue Band campaign had VdBN take its show to customers, which suited the needs of what B. Joseph Pine and James Gilmore refer to as the "experience economy" that has emerged to confront modern business. In this new economy, the basis of economic value changes. For example, consider the progression of value changes shown in the evolution of the birthday cake. In an economy based in agriculture and cottage industry, mothers bought flour, sugar, eggs, butter, and other ingredients to mix and bake birthday cakes. As basic manufacturing industries advanced, Betty Crocker offered premixed ingredients, and cakes were easier to turn out. Later, with bulk manufacturing and the rise of service industry, finished cakes bought from bakeries and grocery stores took over the market. And nowadays, many parents no longer buy cakes but outsource the whole birthday party to Chuck E. Cheese, the Discovery Zone, or some other entertainment establishment. The birthday cake is thrown in with the whole program offered to partygoers. Costs have gone from pennies for ingredients to dollars for cake mixes to tens of dollars for bakery cakes to hundreds of dollars for themed birthday parties. Economic value creation shifted from *extracting* out of naturally occurring resources to *making* standardized products, and then from *delivering* customized products and services to *staging* personalized experiences.

   Business leaders are beginning to see how this progression applies to the way they manage their companies and workforces. The modern age is one of cookbook management, premixed messages, and mass electronic messaging. In this environment, meetings, events, and communications that are customized, personalized, and unique reach people and make them feel special. Employees are the "performers" in the new economy who add value based not only on their knowledge and skills but also on their attitudes and outlook. And they too are consumers in the experience economy and look for meaning, fun, and fulfillment at work as they do in other venues. At VdBN, it became clear that making employees part of the show paid off in increased effort, imagination, and commitment. See B. Joseph Pine and James H. Gilmore, *The Experience Economy: Work Is Theater and Every Business a Stage* (Boston: Harvard Business School Press, 1999).

2. The Fats business team also developed its own roster of best practices:

New Perspective:	Vulnerable Volume, Grow Share
	Connect to Customers
	Grow the Market
New Mindset:	Index 100
	Cut the Tail
New Concepts:	Reposition Powerhouse Brands
	Extend Brands (e.g. sandwiches)
	Functional Foods
New Competitors:	House Brands
New Methods:	Multidisciplinary Account Teams
	Consumer Cookbook Contest
	Retailer's "Big Night" Event

Chapter 11

1. A physics metaphor helps to explain the significance of the cascading. As distance from an object increases, its gravitational forces diminish. The same is true of most organizational change efforts—the further the efforts are from the impetus for change (in this case the chairman and leaders), the weaker the signal and impact. A different force, one that gets stronger as it gets closer to the local application and further from the center, is needed. That alternative force cannot involve compliance and control; instead, it must be one that allows people to inject their own creativity, energy, fun, and improvisation. Replication and cascading needs to strengthen, not weaken, the forces of change and its impact. In VdBN business unit leaders developed and

designed their own cascaded version of outbreaks, learning conferences, team building, restructuring, and accountability. The more closely connected these activities were to the specific local context for change, the more powerful they were for the individuals involved and the local business unit.

2. John P. Kotter, *Leading Change* (Boston: Harvard Business School Press, 1996). See also *Force for Change: How Leadership Differs from Management* (New York: Free Press, 1990) and John P. Kotter and Dan S. Cohen, *The Heart of Change: Real-Life Stories of How People Change Their Organizations* (Boston: Harvard Business School Press, 2002).

3. Team building and TPM were key elements in a larger cultural change in VdBN factories. Factory managers adopted a mix of modern philosophies, training programs, tools and methods to stimulate and steer change. In reflecting on what happened, they described it as purposeful movement from an "old way" of managing a factory to a "new way."

Old Way in Sourcing Units	*New Way in Sourcing Units*
Closely guarded information	Widely shared information
Work = job descriptions	Work = needs of the function
Command and control	Empowerment
Management responsible	Everyone responsible
Mistrust of Works Council	Win-win with Works Council
Pessimistic and dependent	Optimistic and interdependent
No problems discussed	Deal with difficult issues
Tell only good news	No faking

Chapter 12

1. This learning history was a joint effort between a team of action researchers, including authors Philip Mirvis, Karen Ayas, and George Roth along with select leaders on VdBN's side. Every employee in the company, select managers in Unilever, and various suppliers and contractors contributed to the findings. See Appendix 2 for details.

2. The notion that visions can guide a business and provide meaning for its employees is well established. Case studies of long-lived companies in the United States (Kodak, Corning), Asia (Matsushita, Sumitomo), and Europe (Shell, Unilever) stress how a forward-looking perspective has helped to contribute to their longevity. Arie de Geus's *Living Company: Habits for Survival in a Turbulent Business Environment* (Boston: Harvard Business School Press, 2002), developing this idea, contends that clarity of purpose, a capacity to adapt to change, and a cohesive sense of identity all characterize successful companies.

Chapter 13

1. Social scientists use the term *institutionalization* to refer to the aftermath of a transformation—a time when things settle down, new norms become standard operating procedures, and new cultural elements are integrated into the normal way of doing things. Fine in theory. But in the fast-paced world of business, where change seems to be the only constant, this phase of restabilization doesn't last long and is often passed over altogether by the press of further change. See Gerald Zaltman, B. Duncan, and J. Holbek, *Innovations and Organizations* (New York: Wiley Interscience, 1973).

2. The source for quoted remarks in this section is *Inspiration for Growth,* a pamphlet produced by Francisca Jungslager and Maarten van Beek, Unilever, 2002.

3. When talking about the spread of change, social scientists use the term "diffusion" to explain how new ideas and practices move from their original source to other people or groups in a culture. Research on this subject in organizations finds that innovations developed in business units or divisions seldom diffuse to other units and almost never to the corporate center. Some of this has to do with the not-invented-here syndrome that affects adoption of any new practice in companies, no matter how superior it might be to the current approach. And some

has to do with attitudes of superiority in the corporate center. In this case, however, there is evidence that local practices eventually found their way into the corporate center and have since become part and parcel of the Unilever-wide transformation effort. See Everett M. Rogers, *Diffusion of Innovations* (New York: Simon & Schuster, 1996).

4. The acquisition of BestFoods helped on two counts. First, it enabled executives to focus the company's brand portfolio. Second, the subsequent "housecleaning," as one executive described it, removed a number of executives "who were not going to make it happen." The next challenges were to "break the comfort zone" and "bring together management teams" to grow the business.

5. See Karen Ayas and Philip H. Mirvis, "Young Leaders' Forum in Asia: Learning About Leadership, Abundance and Growth," *Reflections* 4, no. 1 (2002): 33–42.

6. See C. K. Prahalad, "Strategies for the Bottom of the Economic Pyramid: India as a Source of Innovation," *Reflections*, 3, no. 4 (2002): 6–14; C. K. Prahalad and Allen Hammond, "Serving the World's Poor, Profitably," *Harvard Business Review* (September 2002).

Chapter 14

1. Peter F. Drucker, "The Theory of the Business," *Harvard Business Review* (September-October 1994): 95–104.

2. See Kurt Lewin, *Resolving Social Conflicts* (New York: Harper-Collins, 1948); William P. Bridges, *Transitions: Making Sense of Life's Changes* (New York: Perseus, 1980); Victor Turner, *Schism and Continuity* (Manchester: Manchester University Press, 1957).

3. See Noel M. Tichy and Mary Ann Devanna, *The Transformational Leader: The Key to Global Competitiveness* (New York: Wiley, 1986).

Chapter 15

1. For a general introduction to the field of performance art in a business context—sometimes called "performativity"—see Marvin Carlson, *Performance* (London: Routledge, 1996).

2. See this idea applied to General Electric's transformation by Noel Tichy and Stratford Sherman, in *Control Your Own Destiny or Someone Else Will*, 2nd ed. (New York: Doubleday Currency, 2001).

3. In this respect, the performance was an occasion for what is termed "cultural reflexivity"—a chance for a culture to look at itself. See Clifford Geertz, *The Interpretation of Cultures* (New York: Harper, 1973).

4. The drama in the Ardennes expressed what anthropologists characterize as a universal drama whereby cultures enact change in the formula of an upheaval, then conflict and reordering, and finally reintegration. See Victor Turner, *Schism and Continuity* (Manchester: Manchester University Press, 1957).

    Two other practical aspects of the Ardennes-as-performance bear comment. First, it meant that Gunning and his top team had to "get their act together" to serve as role models for staff (actors) and to put on a show (producers). Second, in actually performing, they developed and demonstrated their own brand of teamwork and thus became even more effective as a team.

5. See, for example, Peter Vail, *Managing as a Performing Art: New Ideas for a World of Chaotic Change* (San Francisco: Jossey-Bass, 1989); Karen E. Watkins and Victoria J. Marsick, *Sculpting the Learning Organization: Lessons in the Art and Science of Systemic Change* (San Francisco: Jossey-Bass, 1993).

6. See Henry M. Boettinger, "Is Management Really an Art?" *Harvard Business Review* (January February 1975): 54–60; Rosamund Stone Zander and Benjamin Zander, *The Art of Possibility: Transforming Professional and Personal Life* (Boston: Harvard Business School Press, 2000); Philip H. Mirvis,

"Practice Improvisation," *Organization Science* 9, no. 5 (1998): 586–592.

7. See B. Joseph Pine and James H. Gilmore, *The Experience Economy: Work Is Theater and Every Business a Stage* (Boston: Harvard Business School Press, 1999).

Chapter 16

1. See Daniel Goleman, *Emotional Intelligence: Why It Can Matter More Than IQ* (New York: Bantam, 1995).
2. See William A. Kahn, "To Be Fully There: Psychological Presence at Work," *Human Relations* 45, no. 4 (1992): 321–349; also Douglas T. Hall and Philip H. Mirvis, "The New Protean Career: Psychological Success and the Path with a Heart," in *The Career Is Dead—Long Live the Career*, edited by D. T. Hall and Associates (San Francisco: Jossey-Bass, 1996).
3. Research by Michael Learner and colleagues suggest that human "meaning" needs cannot be met solely by making work more intellectually engaging. Indeed, their studies find that what middle-class blue- and white-collar workers bemoan most is the absence of love and care in the workplace and any connection between their jobs and larger purpose in life. See Michael Learner, *The Politics of Meaning* (Reading, Mass.: Addison-Wesley, 1996).
4. See Peter Senge, "Communities of Commitment: The Heart of the Learning Organization," *Organization Dynamics* (Fall 1993); Kaz Gozdz (ed.), *Community Building in Business* (San Francisco: New Leaders Press, 1996); Philip H. Mirvis, "Community Building in Business," *Reflections* 3, no. 3 (2002): 45–51.
5. Fred E. Fiedler and Martin M. Chemers, *Improving Leadership Effectiveness: The Leader Match Concept* (New York: Wiley, 1983).
6. Noel M. Tichy and Eli Cohen, *The Leadership Engine: How Winning Companies Build Leaders at Every Level* (New York: HarperInformation, 1997).

7. See Senge, *The Fifth Discipline: The Art and Practice of the Learning Organization.*

8. Tom J. Peters and Robert H. Waterman, *In Search of Excellence* (New York: HarperCollins, 1982); Ken Smith and David N. Berg, *Paradoxes of Group Life* (San Francisco: Jossey-Bass, 1987); Robert E. Quinn, *Beyond Rational Management* (San Francisco: Jossey-Bass, 1988); Shona L. Brown and Kathleen M. Eisenhardt, *Competing on the Edge: Strategy as Structured Chaos* (Boston: Harvard Business School Press, 1998).

9. This, in theoretical terms, is the way "complex adaptive systems" create order at the "edge of chaos." Several variants of the "new science" speak to this dynamic. The order to be found in chaos, for instance, revolves around an aptly named "strange attractor"; Margaret Wheatley suggests that its equivalent in social systems is *meaning*. Social scientists can draw "maps" of these processes and attribute adaptation to the harmonious co-evolution of psychic, social, and material forces. To others, such notions of an implicate order come from the field of inquiry known as "spiritual science" where, it is presumed, mind and matter coevolve and interpenetrate in an unseen order. See Margaret J. Wheatley, *Leadership and the New Science: Learning About Organization from an Orderly Universe* (San Francisco: Berrett-Koehler, 1993), and Willis Harman and John Hormann, *Creative Work* (Indianapolis: Knowledge Systems, 1990).

10. Mary Jo Hatch, "Exploring the Empty Spaces of Organizing: How Improvisational Jazz Helps Redescribe Organization Structure," *Organization Studies* (Winter 1999); John Kao, *Jamming: The Art and Discipline of Business Creativity* (New York: Harper-Business, 1995); David B. Yoffie and Mary Kwak, *Judo Strategy: Turning Your Competitor's Strength to Your Advantage* (Boston: Harvard Business School Press, 2001).

11. In literature, see Arthur Koestler, *The Act of Creation* (New York: Macmillan, 1964); poetry, see David Whyte, *The Heart Aroused* (New York: Doubleday, 1994); creative arts, see S. Arieti, *Creativity* (New York: Basic Books, 1976); sports and medicine, see

Bernie Siegel, *Love, Medicine and Miracles* (New York: Harper-Collins, 1986); Mihaly Csikszentmihalyi, *Flow: The Psychology of Optimal Experience* (New York: HarperCollins, 1990).

12. In an evocative essay, Diana Whitney describes spirit variously as energy, as meaning, and as epistemology. Her illustrations come from Native American traditions, Chinese medicine, the myths of the new science, and the musings of organizational scientists trying to make sense of the forces that impinge on themselves and those they study. In many cultures, she notes, spirit is also sacred. See Diana Whitney, "Spirituality as a Global Organizing Potential," *Reflections* 3, no. 3 (2002): 76–85; also Deepak Chopra, *Quantum Healing: Exploring the Frontiers of Mind Body Medicine* (New York: Bantam Books, 1989), and Thich Nhat Hahn, *The Miracle of Mindfulness* (Berkeley, Calif.: Parallax Press, 1990).

13. See Jay Conger and Associates, *Spirit at Work: Discovering the Spirituality in Leadership* (San Francisco: Jossey-Bass, 1994); Lee Bolman and Terry Deal, *Leading with Soul: An Uncommon Journey of Spirit* (San Francisco: Jossey-Bass, 1995); and Joseph Jaworski, *Synchronicity: The Inner Path of Leadership* (San Francisco: Berrett-Koehler, 1996). On spiritual dimensions of contemporary leadership, see Robert Greenleaf, "The Leader as Servant," in *In the Company of Others: Making Community in a Modern World*, edited by Claude Whitmyer (New York: Putnam, 1993); Max DePree, *Leadership Is an Art* (New York: Doubleday, 1989); and Stephen Covey, *Principle-Centered Leadership* (New York: Summit, 1990).

14. See the classic formulation in psychological terms by P. Watzlawick, J. Weakland, and R. Fisch, *Change: Principles of Problem Formation and Problem Resolution* (New York: Norton, 1974); its implication for managing organizational change by Donald N. Michael and Philip H. Mirvis, "Changing Erring and Learning," in *Failures in Organization Development and Change*, edited by P. Mirvis and D. Berg (New York: Wiley Interscience, 1977).

15. See Philip H. Mirvis, "The Art of Assessing the Quality of Work Life," in *Organizational Assessment*, edited by E. Lawler, D. Nadler, and C. Cammann (New York: Wiley, 1980).

16. See Michael Polanyi, Harry Prosch, and Kevin Prosch, *Meaning* (Chicago: University of Chicago Press, 1977).

17. Conflicts between action and research are commonplace and create their share of dilemmas. The twist here is that in Jordan and at VdBN's learning conference, we ourselves were part of the show. We were assuming roles, performing on stage, had license to dramatize, and had effects we wanted to achieve. Clearly this is not the norm for fieldwork, and our participation in staging a meaningful event no doubt influenced the way we saw things and reported on them afterward. In that way our experience is parallel to that of staff and managers at VdBN. And we have to check our own biases in reporting what happened in the company and what is to be learned. See Philip H. Mirvis, "Managing Research Whilst Researching Managers," in *Organizational Culture*, edited by P. Frost, L. Moore, M. Louis, C. Lundberg, and J. Martin (Thousand Oaks, Calif.: Sage, 1985).

18. Marketers and advertisers know how to get people's attention, gain a positive disposition toward their product or service, and induce the consumer to buy and use it. The work involves gaining mindshare (head) and appealing to emotions (heart) that people can associate with their product. These same principles were applied in developing messages and using media for development, learning, and change at VdBN. In an increasingly cluttered organizational life, executives need to grab the attention of managers and workers, inspire them to be more focused and productive, and help them change for the better.

Does it make sense for a company like VdBN to spend huge amounts of money to travel to Ardennes, Scotland, the Sinai, Israel, and Jordan? Or to bear the production costs of staging learning conferences for eighteen hundred people? It might, if you consider that these costs are for generating an environment in which the information that is delivered grows and thrives, or for creating a medium that allows you to capture the hearts and minds of people. Inspirational, unfamiliar settings and activities create new opportunities for reaching people in ways unavailable in the day-to-day office or factory setting. VdBN found an innovative way to deliver its message—a legacy of growth—and the way in which it delivered that message was as important as the message itself.

Appendix 2

1. George Roth and Art Kleiner, *Car Launch: The Human Side of Managing Change* (Oxford, England: Oxford University Press, 2000); Art Kleiner and George Roth, *Oil Change: Perspectives in Corporate Transformation* (Oxford, England: Oxford University Press, 2000); Art Kleiner and George Roth, "How to Make Experience Your Company's Best Teacher," *Harvard Business Review* 75, no. 5 (September-October 1997).

2. Adjacent to the narrative there is commentary written to help the reader reflect on why a particular quote was chosen and what it might mean. The learning history document given to people at VdBN contained such commentary. It is sprinkled through this manuscript and appears in the text as appropriate.

Acknowledgments

This story of VdBN's transformation and the growth of its leaders is a tribute to the men and women who led the changes that it records. It has been our privilege to observe, participate, interview, and work with all of them. Had they not all engaged and embraced dramatic changes, there would be no story to tell. We were invited not only to study the transformation process but also to play a part in the drama of events and to see and experience firsthand the warmth, caring, and collegiality that the people of VdBN had for one another.

The company, and Unilever, reflecting Dutch character, gave us the freedom to "tell it like we saw it." Everyone we asked, without exception, shared their thoughts with us. Our gratitude goes foremost to Tex Gunning. He led the transformation from 1995 to 2000, developed a cadre of young leaders, engaged the workforce, and encouraged this learning history. He was generous with his time and thinking, open and responsive to our questions, receptive to our ideas and challenges.

We are grateful to Anthonie Stal, the new chairman, who supported our efforts in concluding our study and provided continued access.

As in any performance, where many people are required backstage to create the show, numerous people—a cast of hundreds—played a part in producing this book and our gratitude goes to every one of them. Ria Messer and Laura Tan, our support team early on, helped us in getting started, setting up interviews, and making sure we had what we needed. A team led by Jaap Kalma and including Neil Wickers and Rob Schaerlaeckens championed the learning history process—serving as data gatherers and interpreters, reading and reviewing manuscripts, discussing what we learned. Hans Cornuit was always there for us with insights from his HR leadership position.

We want to acknowledge all those from VdBN who assisted us in our research and writing. Perhaps those that endured us best were the young leaders and experienced executives whom we interviewed and questioned extensively—Hans Synhaeve, Marijn van Tiggelen, Aart-Jan van Triest, Mick van Ettinger, Ad van Oers, Roef van Duin, Janti Soeripto, Conny Braams, Bauke Rouwers, Evert Bos, Geert Maassen, Gert-Jan de Geus, Rein Ettema, Hans van't Sant, Elly Zwaal, Hans Mikkelsen, Leon Schoofs, Gerard Prins, and many others. They not only made themselves available, but also helped us with access to their people. Jose Cavanna, Nancy Isaacs, Eric Jan de Rooij, David Saunders, and a team from (then) Andersen Consulting were among those outsiders who shared with us their experiences with VdBN.

Our gratitude also goes to researchers Renate Kenter from University of Nijenrode, who helped with the organization and analysis of more than four thousand pages of interview material, and Anne Kegan from Erasmus University Rotterdam, who conducted interviews.

In the process of writing a manuscript, it is always helpful to have opportunities to talk about it as a work in progress. We are thankful to Arjan Overwater from Unilever and to the S4 group at the Society for Organizational Learning who provided venues to distill lessons learned. Thanks also to Jane Gebhart, Ed Schein, and Bill Torbert for their editorial and substantive comments on the article we wrote from these materials for the journal *Reflections*.

We extend our deepest appreciation to Leslie Stephen, who recrafted the original manuscript into this book, bringing her intelligence, passion, care, and love to the story. Our thanks also go, for their support and expertise, to Susan Williams, Byron Schneider, Rob Brandt, and the rest of the team at Jossey-Bass and the parent company Wiley.

And, of course, those whom we needed most backstage were our families and friends. Their forbearance allowed us to be absorbed in this tale, to experience and tell this extraordinary business adventure in detail. Thank you for being there for us as we traveled to the desert and back and spent the many days on the road and writing.

About the Authors

Philip Mirvis is an organizational psychologist whose research and private consulting centers on large-scale organizational change and the impact of company life on people. A regular contributor to journals, he has authored eight books including *The Cynical Americans* and *Joining Forces*.

Mirvis has designed breakthrough corporate events involving theater, painting, sculpture, and mask making, orchestrated rituals for merging companies, and led outdoor team building in the Rockies, Pyrenees, Alps, and Himalayas. Multisector experiences include community service in the urban United States, Paris, and London, as well as among aboriginal peoples in Borneo and Australia, plus a variety of community dialogues on environmental and socioeconomic issues. Business clients include Ben & Jerry's, Unisys, Royal Dutch Shell, Hexcel, Lotus, GE Information Systems, Hewlett-Packard, Ford, and Chemical Bank.

Mirvis is a fellow of the Center for Corporate Citizenship and Work Family Roundtable and has been board cochair of the Foundation for Community Encouragement. He has a B.A. from Yale University and a Ph.D. from the University of Michigan. He has taught at Boston University, Jiao Tong University in Shanghai, China, and the London Business School, and is adjunct faculty for the University of Michigan's Graduate School of Business. He has three daughters and lives in Bethesda, Maryland.

Karen Ayas is a founding partner of the Ripples Group, a management consulting practice specializing in growth strategies and change management. She is on the faculty of Rotterdam School of Management, Erasmus University, and adjunct faculty in Babson College. She has published numerous articles on change management, organization design, project management, and leadership. Her most recent book, *Design for Learning for Innovation*, comes from her longtime research in the Netherlands.

Ayas has been an HR director of a major hospital in Israel, and has consulted intensively in the telecom, aircraft, and consumer goods industries. She has a Ph.D. in management of technology from Erasmus University Rotterdam (the Netherlands), and holds B.S. and M.S. degrees from Technion, Israel Institute of Technology. She is on the Board of Trustees of the Society for Organizational Learning and is associate editor of *Reflections* (a journal on learning and change published by MIT Press). She now lives in Newton, Massachusetts, with her son and husband.

George Roth is a researcher at MIT's Sloan School of Management and executive director of the Ford-MIT Alliance. He writes about companies' experiences in developing and transforming themselves through the exchange of knowledge. He is a coauthor of *The Dance of Change: The Challenges to Sustain Momentum in Learning Organizations; Car Launch: Managing the Human Side of Change*; and *Oil Change: Perspectives on Corporate Transformation*.

Roth has served as research director for the MIT Center for Organizational Learning and is a founding member of the Society for Organizational Learning. He is also cofounder of Reflection Learning Associates, Inc., a consulting firm specializing in helping individuals and organizations change and learn from their experience. Clients include Ford Motor Company, General Motors, Boeing, Shell Oil, British Petroleum, Mobil Oil, Philips, Siemens, Intel, Hewlett-Packard, Harley Davidson, Herman Miller, and Arthur D. Little.

Prior to his academic career, Roth worked for a decade at Digital Equipment Corporation in the United States and Europe, holding various line management positions. He has a Ph.D. in organizational studies, an M.B.A. in marketing and finance, and a B.S. in mechanical engineering. Hobbies include sailing, running, and skiing, and keeping up with his wife and two energetic teenage daughters at home in Maine.

Index

251